9913
F

P9-CKA-225

LASTING ATTACHMENTS

Best wishes,
Annette Sanford

Southwest Life and Letters

A series designed to publish outstanding new fiction and nonfiction about Texas and the American Southwest and to present classic works of the region in handsome new editions.

General Editors: Suzanne Comer, Southern Methodist University Press; Tom Pilkington, Tarleton State University.

ANNETTE SANFORD

LASTING ATTACHMENTS

Southern Methodist University Press

DALLAS

Copyright © 1989 by Annette Sanford
All rights reserved
Printed in the United States of America

First edition, 1989
Requests for permission to reproduce material
from this work should be sent to:

Rights and Permissions
Southern Methodist University Press
Box 415; Dallas, Texas 75275

LIBRARY OF CONGRESS CATALOGING-IN-PUBLICATION DATA

Sanford, Annette.
Lasting attachments / Annette Sanford.
p.   cm.—(Southwest life and letters)
ISBN 0-87074-284-1: $12.95
I. Title.   II. Series.
PS3569.H5792L37   1989
813'.54—dc19   88-39065
CIP

A number of the stories in this collection appeared first in other
publications, sometimes in a slightly different form: "Happy Fortieth,
Ed and Shirley" and "Harvest" in *North American Review*; "The Girls
in the Garden" (as "Grandmother's Little Girl") in *Redbook*; "Six
White Horses" and "Limited Access" in *The Ohio Review*; "Living"
(as "Living with Lura") in *Yankee*; "Trip in a Summer Dress" in
Prairie Schooner; "Twilight" in *Story Quarterly*; "Standing By" (as
"My Mother, My Friend") in *McCall's*. "Living" is reprinted with
permission from *Yankee Publishing*.

These stories are works of fiction. Names, characters, places, and
incidents are either the product of the author's imagination or are
used fictitiously. Any resemblance to actual events, locales, or
persons, living or dead, is entirely coincidental.

Design by Molly Renda

For Lukey and Anna

The author is grateful to the National Endowment for the Arts for making this work possible.

Contents

LASTING ATTACHMENTS

Happy Fortieth, Ed and Shirley

Ed and Shirley turned up again this morning, on the garage floor this time. Harry and I were backing out to go spend the day with his sister Benedict when I remembered that I hadn't finished covering up the pansies.

"Wait a minute," I said. "The plant I left out is the nicest one in the batch, and it may be freezing by the time we come home."

Harry said, "Do you want me to do it?"

"I'll get it." I went back in the garage and that's when I spotted Ed and Shirley. I suppose they fell out of the overhead cabinet when I was bringing down the Christmas decorations. Or maybe all winter they've been stuck there under the washer, waiting to make themselves useful for once.

Anyway, the folder they're pasted into was just the right size to fill a gap in a soup box. I put the box on top of my plant and a flowerpot on top of the box and got back in the car.

I told Harry what I'd done. "And I'm not going to feel guilty."

"Good," he said. "Don't."

"You never wanted me to throw them away before."

"You're not throwing them away now."

"They'll be ruined out in the weather all day."

Harry said, "They're only clutter anyway. Isn't that your theory?"

I admitted it was. Down with clutter: jars without lids, frying pans without handles, pictures of people nobody knows.

The first time Ed and Shirley showed up was New Year's Day, 1957. I spent all morning putting together a coconut cream pie and then I walked off to the corner with Harry to watch for the Knights of Columbus float his boss was riding and burned the whole thing up. When we came back, smoke met us at the front door. Inside the oven frizzles of coconut flared like Roman candles. We were still fanning the smell out when we sat down in the living room after lunch to look through a box of family mementos Benedict had brought over.

"This is the last of the stuff from Mama's house," Benedict said and dumped in front of us a mixture of odds and ends spanning three generations: collar buttons and tintypes, engraved calling cards and dozens of prints from the box cameras of the thirties. There was a porcelain shaving dish with hard yellow soap cracked in the bottom and a stack of foxed Valentines so lacy and sweet I couldn't get enough of them.

What caught Harry's eye was a photographer's folder, gray and stiff-backed, with embossed scrolls twined around the edges. Glued inside were a couple of sepia-toned studio prints of a young man and woman.

Harry laughed. "Look at this guy's ears. I bet on a clear night he could pick up Chicago."

I was more interested in his peculiar taste in clothes. "Who are they?"

Harry didn't know. "Ask Ben."

Benedict didn't know either, but her guess was that they were a couple of the roomers who tracked in and out of their mother's house during the war years while Ben was in the WAACs and Harry and I were in Texas. "What does the inscription say?"

I read aloud the inky scrawl. "Love, Ed and Shirley."

Benedict went back to inspecting an infant version of herself as bare as an egg on a white fur rug. "Didn't Uncle Fox Warner have a son named Ed?"

Harry said, "He had a son named Fred who departed this vale of tears in 1920."

I remember Ben snickering. "In 1920, Lucille. Harry was told ahead of time that the question might come up and wrote the date inside his shirt cuff."

Harry said, "Every Cemetery Clean-Up Day until I was fourteen I ate my lunch on Fred Warner's tombstone."

Ed and Shirley, I observed, were a jazzy-looking couple out of the forties. The Golden Era. I felt my Frank Sinatra goosebumps rising on my spine. "Look at Shirley's pompadour. Look at all that dark lipstick."

In 1944 I looked something like Shirley myself, except that I was sixteen and she was more like twenty—and my lips were thin and anxious-looking and hers were a sassy Cupid's bow, generous and kissable. I don't mind telling you, that picture took me back.

I said to Benedict, "Don't you wish you knew who the girl is?"

"She's Ed's wife," Harry said.

Benedict said, "Thanks for clearing up muddy water. Now you can tell us who Ed is."

Harry had found a gold pocket watch he thought he

could make run again. "I can tell you who he isn't—Uncle Fox Warner's son."

Benedict went off with her boyfriend that afternoon— an ice cream salesman who eventually became her second husband. She left the mementos behind, scattered all over my rug. Putting them back in the box I got moony over Shirley.

"She's pregnant," I said to Harry.

Pregnancy was not our best subject. "All you can see is her head, Lucille."

"Her head is enough. See how milky-looking she is around the eyes?"

"You'd be milky-looking too if you weren't but twenty and your husband had lost the best part of his hair."

Harry isn't a vain man but if he's proud of anything it's what grows on his head. "A receding hairline can't hold a candle to that polka dot shirt and flowered tie."

Harry reminded me, "Guys in the army liked to wear flashy civvies whenever they got a chance."

I said I doubted if Ed was in the service. "I bet as soon as he got his draft notice he went around the barn and shot his toe off."

Harry laughed. "You're pretty hard on old Ed."

"Ed was hard on Shirley, getting her pregnant in the middle of a war."

The delicate truth I was ironically referring to was that Harry had gotten me pregnant in the middle of the same war. I wasn't finished with high school and the next thing I knew I was Private Warner's wife sharing a boardinghouse room with two older ladies outside an air force base in Texas. Camp followers, some people called us. I lost the baby. It ejected without ceremony onto an examining table in a San Antonio clinic. The doctor let me put my skirt back on and walk out of there. Naturally an infection set in, calling a halt to all future babies. I went on following Harry, though. There wasn't much else I could do. School was out and I hadn't graduated.

On the way to Benedict's I said to Harry, "I should have found something else to cover up the pansy plant."

"It's nothing to worry about," he said. "Just forget it."

But I couldn't forget it. "In 1944 Ed put out a chunk of money for those pictures of him and Shirley."

"He was a gambler, you've always insisted, with money running out of his ears."

I've never been fond of Ed. He has a weak look. But I've never been crazy about Shirley either. I don't trust a woman who counts too much on being pretty, as Shirley plainly does or she never would have been photographed in that coy pose looking over her shoulder. Still, it was a mistake tossing them out in the cold, exposing two dressed-up people to the possibility of sleet and the lifted hind legs of the neighborhood dogs.

Harry got tired of listening to me fret. "Stop worrying," he said. "It's not as if they were friends of ours."

I was shocked at Harry. "You can't say they're strangers."

After New Year's Day 1957, Harry and I moved every two or three months, snailtracking across the Oklahoma oil fields. Mixed in with the necessary junk we dragged around the country was Benedict's box of mementos. She was in school then, renting a cramped little room, and later she was divorced and living in an efficiency apartment. I guess most people have a box like that, stuff they don't want but can't get rid of.

Eventually I stopped being surprised when I pulled out a drawer and found Ed and Shirley lounging around inside. But it always rankled me that those two had a child growing up about the same age as ours would have been if somebody had revoked that quack doctor's license.

Ever so often I'd say to Harry, "These people aren't even kin to us. I'm pitching them out."

Harry would say, "Let's wait awhile." Or, "What's the point after fifteen years?"

After twenty years he said, "Tossing them out now would be a sacrilege."

I let him get away with that half-baked opinion until we

bought our house last year and settled down in Chickasha. Then I sorted through everything, and while Harry was mowing the lawn I filled a trash can.

In a little while he came out to the kitchen. "Guess what blew off the back end of the garbage truck?"

Like a simpleton I cried. All those years. I was never going to be rid of them.

"You think Shirley's cute, don't you?" I burst out. "Ever since you saw her you've been wishing it was her you were married to instead of me."

Harry couldn't bridge the gap fast enough to say boo.

"Go on!" I hollered, as uncertain again as a bride of sixteen. "Do what you've been dying to do—give them a page in the family album."

He got on his high horse. "They're nothing special to me."

"You dragged them back in the house, didn't you?"

"Cars were running over them!"

I should have been awarded an Oscar for the way I pranced off to the living room and rigged up a shrine. On top of the piano I arranged a vase of artificial nasturtiums beside Ed and Shirley and let the milk glass lamp beam lovingly down on their dumb, placid faces. The preacher's wife across the street saw the light burning and trotted over for a chat.

Harry told her, "These are Lucille's cousins, Mrs. Bert-ner. The salt of the earth. They're missionaries in Africa."

The fight we had afterward was the best thing that ever happened to us. It cleared the air back to the start of World War II. Early in the morning, lying alongside Harry I told him, "It'll serve you right if the church takes up a love offering for Ed and Shirley."

Harry chucked me under my second chin. "It'll serve us both right. We'll take a trip to Hawaii."

Benedict, who is single for the third time, served us roast beef with horseradish today. I would have preferred gravy. After dinner she reminisced in the pine-paneled den the ice cream salesman built her.

"Does anybody remember the Christmas Lucille caught fire to the coconut pie?"

"It was New Year's," I said. "1957."

Harry said, "Lucille was told beforehand that the question might come up and wrote the date inside her cuff."

Ben frowned. "What do you mean, Harry?"

"I think he's quoting your joke. The afternoon the pie burned up."

She didn't recall making a joke. "What I remember is that picture of me naked on a fur rug—and Gracey and her husband."

"Who?" I said.

"The girl with the pompadour. The guy with the ears that could pick up Chicago. Did I ever tell you I was right about those two? They did rent rooms at Mama's. I asked Putter McAdoo."

Putter McAdoo was a hometown boy who really did go behind the barn and shoot his toe off, so he was around through the whole war to get acquainted with the tenants in Mother Warner's house.

"It wasn't Gracey," I said. "Shirley was her name. Shirley and Ed."

Ben's look was skeptical. "Shirley? Are you sure? Well, it doesn't matter—they got killed anyway."

"Who?" I said.

"The couple we're talking about, Lucille. Gracey or Shirley, and what's-his-name."

"Killed?" Harry looked green. "Who told you so?"

"Putter McAdoo. Isn't anybody listening?"

"When?" I said.

"Ten or twelve years ago. I went out with him for awhile between Clinton and Joseph."

My mouth got awfully dry. "I mean when were they killed?"

"Sometime during the war. They were moving from

Mama's and a train hit their car down along the Louisiana border."

"A train." I turned around to Harry. "That stupid Ed. He ran their car up on a railroad track."

Harry said, "Who was driving, Ben?"

"Does it make any difference, for God's sake? It was forty years ago."

"There could have been a fog, Lucille. Or they might have had the windows rolled up and the radio on."

I said, "Don't tell me what happened. He gambled on beating that train."

"Shirley could have been driving."

"Harry," I said, "Shirley was six months pregnant."

When we turned in our driveway the car lights picked up the square shape of the soup box. Everything around it that wasn't covered looked stiff and frozen.

"I'll get out here," I said. "I'm going to bring the pictures inside."

Harry rolled on toward the garage. "Don't, Lucille. I don't want you to."

"I feel as bad as you do, Harry."

"Then you know we'd feel worse if we looked at the pictures."

"Harry, listen. Ben could have had the wrong couple. She called Shirley 'Gracey.' The only thing Putter had to go on was her description. Think how many girls with pompadours could have lived at your mother's. Think how many guys have ears as big as Ed's."

"Ben could have been right, though."

"If they were really dead do you think all these years we wouldn't have known it?"

Harry stopped the car and shut off the motor. "I do have the feeling they might be living somewhere close by. In Tulsa maybe. Or over in Ardmore."

"So do I, Harry." I pecked him on the cheek. "Let's go get the pictures."

"Ben would think we're crazy."

"Ben is incapable of lasting attachments."

The Girls in the Garden

The sun shines on Jeanette and me. We are wearing our Easter dresses and long white socks. I have on pink shoes and Jeanette has a barrette shaped like a rainbow in her hair.

My grandmother directs Boris from the porch. "Pose them over there, please," Mam says. "In front of the flowers with their baskets of eggs." She shades her eyes with the front section of the *Lake Nelson News*.

"That's lovely, girls," she calls out to us. "Now give us a big smile."

Jeanette and I are twelve. Well, almost. We are ten and a half. I am happy because I won the egg hunt. But I would be happier if my best friend and I were wearing puff-sleeved organdy dresses instead of eighty percent polyester, and if we had satin bows in our hair the same as my mother and her best friend have in the picture in Mam's album taken when *they* were twelve. If we were wearing lipstick and training bras, I would be happier still.

Boris is pointing the camera our way, so I poke Jeanette in the side. "Put your arm around my waist, and don't smile your sick chicken smile."

Boris says, "Ready?" We aren't, but he snaps the picture anyway.

Boris is my mother's new husband. He came as a big surprise to Mam and me. We had never heard of him until my mother brought him to meet us yesterday. We were still thinking her boyfriend was Michael, the one who was teaching her how to walk.

My mother is a model, or she will be when she gets her break and can stop handing out menus at the Plantation Palms. There is always something blocking your way when you are trying for a career. My mother says you have to decide what is most productive and put that first. That's why I live here with Mam, and my mother lives in Dallas.

"I have to be able to jump up and run when my agent calls," she explained to me once. "There wouldn't be time to go hunting for a sitter."

Right now my mother is inside the house talking on the

phone to my father, who lives in Parks Grove, Tennessee, with his new wife. Mam has brought the rest of us out here to take pictures and smell the sweet peas and the four o'clocks and to keep Boris from seeing my mother get upset.

Mam sent Boris out first and then she said, "This is not a good time to air dirty linen, Iris."

My mother said to her, "Why shouldn't Boris be in on everything?"

Mam answered, "If you don't know by now, there's no use telling you."

My mother is beautiful, like the flower she is named for. She is tall and delicate-looking with pale white skin. I am short and square-looking with freckles on my nose. But maybe I'm lucky. Mam says life is more complicated if you have to deal with being gorgeous on top of everything else.

Boris fiddles with his camera. It is the very same one he uses to take pictures of models for magazines. Mam calls from the porch, "If it's not too much trouble, take one more of the girls, please. Just to be on the safe side."

Boris is wearing a white shirt with the cuffs turned back and the pants to the gray suit he wore when he took me to pick up Jeanette before church. He wants to change into shorts and go skiing at the lake. Jeanette and I want to go too, but my aunt and uncle are coming soon with their baby and we can't leave. Boris's car is too small for all of us anyway, a sports model with just enough room for my mother and him.

I won't really mind if they go off and leave us. That way Jeanette and I can talk more about marriage and try to imagine how sex is done.

"It's gross thinking about it," Jeanette whispered when we were setting the table before lunch.

"It's how babies are made," I told her. "If you want a baby you have to get used to it."

"I won't," Jeanette said. "I'll order my baby out of a catalog."

Mam calls to Boris again. "Come sit in the shade, won't you?"

She makes room for him beside her on the swing. I know by the way she doesn't quite look at him that she wishes he was someone else. I sit down by Jeanette on the steps and try to figure out who. Not my father, I know, although Mam never says anything bad about him.

When I was smaller I used to ask Mam, "What is he like?"

"He's handsome," she always said. "You have his eyes."

Yesterday, before we knew my mother was bringing any-one with her, I said, "Why did my father divorce my mother?"

Mam said, "He wasn't happy being married."

"He's married now."

"Now he's older and more settled."

When I ask her why my father lets months go by without sending me my check, Mam says maybe he doesn't have it. She says I should never confuse a small amount of money with a large amount of love.

That's what Mam and I have, a large amount of love. She says we are like two peas in a pod in our white house with the white fence around it. We have two bedrooms and a bigger room for company that she calls the parlor. We also have this little pocket-handkerchief garden with pebble pathways instead of a lawn because Mam can't mow grass and I shouldn't try because I'm not twelve yet.

We lead a quiet life, Mam tells people when they ask about us. We play Parcheesi on a speckled old board. In my room at school I'm the only one who knows how. For dessert on Saturdays we split Snickers bars. We put old socks on our hands and polish the furniture and make out our grocery lists on the backs of used envelopes. On cold nights we dress in our nightgowns right after supper. We eat popcorn and Mam takes down her hair and reads to me out of books with the covers falling off. The children in the books say things like "Mary Alice has a suitor who will call within a fortnight." None of them have ever heard of TV.

When I told Jeanette she said, "No cartoons?" and fell over backward on the floor.

Boris checks his watch. Mam says politely, "You must tell me again where you and Iris live."

"In Brookwood." Boris shows a lot of straight teeth and tells her it's a subdivision.

"They live in a condominium," I put in, so Jeanette will know. Last night my mother slept with me in my bed and told me all about it, to reassure me, she said. So now I reassure Jeanette. "There's a sauna and an exercise club, but the management doesn't allow children."

Boris clears his throat. "Later, when we're more settled, we'll probably look for something else."

Mam says she understands perfectly. I understand more than Mam does. At breakfast when she went out to the kitchen to get more toast Boris told my mother he was bitten in the night by an upholstery tack. "That's some couch," he said.

"Oh, poor love, I'll make it up to you," my mother answered and kissed him on the mouth. I could never kiss Boris on the mouth, not even to get a baby.

"Iris likes the condominium setup in Brookwood," Boris says to Mam. "She has a maid three times a week."

"What does the maid do?" I ask.

Boris laughs. "Whatever Iris doesn't want to."

I tell Jeanette, "Won't it be fun, getting letters from the maid!"

"Liddy, you and Jeanette may serve the ice cream now," Mam says suddenly.

We both jump up, but at the door I remember. "Aunt Tia and Uncle Bob and Rodney aren't here."

"We won't wait," Mam says. "The baby may nap."

I explain to Jeanette. "If Rodney falls asleep, they wait for him to wake up before they put him in his car seat. If they don't, he might get—what is that word, Mam?"

"Disoriented."

"Would you like chocolate revel?" I ask Boris. "Or creamy pecan praline?"

Boris stands up and stretches. "I'd rather have a beer."

After we bring everyone's dessert, my mother finishes her telephone call and comes out on the porch. I love her dress. It's thin and has lots of colors, like butterfly wings. She walks on her high heels the way Michael taught her and starts talking before she even tastes her ice cream.

"I told him I'd give him one more month and then I'm hauling him into court."

Mam says, "How nice you could reach him, Iris. Aren't the four o'clocks bright and pretty?"

"I told him flat out that Boris will not put up with late payments. Liddy is his child and he can't expect another man to buy clothes for her and put food in her mouth."

I cross my legs and pray hard I won't wet my pants. Mam doesn't look at me. "We'll discuss it later, Iris."

"You can't imagine how furious he makes me!"

Mam says, "Boris was telling us that in Brookside you have a maid."

"It's Brook*wood*, Mam. Brookside is that tacky little town way down on the coast."

Boris is smoking long brown cigarettes. "Iris," he says, "if we're going out on the lake—"

My mother flutters her hands. "Yes, darling, go ahead and change." She touches Mam's arm. "Will it be all right? Or will Tia think I'm snubbing her?"

I ask out loud, "What does 'snubbing' mean?"

"Go ahead whenever you're ready," Mam says. "You remember how it is with a baby. You can't plan what time you'll arrive anywhere."

I tell Jeanette, "Rodney is the cutest thing when he gets up from his nap. All smiles and no teeth."

Boris comes out again skinny-legged in white shorts, carrying the suitcases. He thinks they should go straight home from the lake because of the traffic. My mother thinks so too. She kisses us all, even Jeanette.

"We'll see you soon, Mam."

We stand at the gate and wave goodbye until they turn the corner. I tell Jeanette, "When I get married I'll probably have a black sports car."

"Mine will be white with red bucket seats," Jeanette says.

Jeanette and I each have another dish of ice cream and then Aunt Tia and Uncle Bob and Rodney arrive. You would never believe Aunt Tia is my mother's sister. She looks more like me, except her hair is frizzier and her freckles are brighter. She laughs a lot. She is always saying, "Here, let me help you with that," and putting her arms around you, the way Mam does.

Uncle Bob carries Rodney around on his hip while he looks at the pictures on the wall and eats peanuts from the bowl on the coffee table.

I take Jeanette off in the corner. "Do you think it would be gross making a baby with him?"

She looks over my shoulder. "Maybe they adopted it."

Aunt Tia brings coffee into the parlor. "I think Iris might at least have mentioned that she was planning to get married."

Mam says, "It was a sudden decision."

"That's why we have telephones. What's Boris like?"

I know the answer and speak up first. "He's going to like being married."

Mam says, "Iris seems happy."

"Except with my father," I explain to Aunt Tia. "She isn't happy with him."

Aunt Tia looks at Mam and lifts her eyebrows. "Money again?"

Mam nods. She says to Uncle Bob, "Boris left beer."

Aunt Tia looks at me. "Sugar, when are you coming to see us?" She smiles at Jeanette. "You come too. We'll have a good time."

Jeanette and I hug each other. "Can we take care of Rodney?"

"You bet you can." Aunt Tia winks at Mam. "You can change his diapers and everything."

Jeanette is the next one to leave. Just before dark she goes off with her brother who lifeguards at the country club. He picks her up wearing a big blob of white ointment on the end of his nose.

Aunt Tia and Uncle Bob eat the leftovers from lunch and then they leave too, with Rodney in his car seat.

It isn't winter, but right after we do the dishes Mam takes down her hair and we put on our nightgowns.

I sit in her lap in the old white rocker. "Am I too big for this?"

She puts her talcum-scented cheek next to mine. "You won't be too big until the chair falls to pieces."

We listen to the mockingbirds out on the telephone wire. They don't care if it's dark. *Trilly-hoo, trilly-ha, tiddle-diddle, blue one.*

I ask Mam, "Why didn't you like Boris?"

"I didn't have time to find out whether I liked him or not," she says.

"He's in love with my mother," I tell her. "I mean he's always wanting her to kiss him the way they do on TV."

Mam nods her head. "I did catch on to that."

I slide down her legs and get the photograph album off the sewing machine. Then I settle again in the snuggly place between Mam's breasts.

"Let's look at my favorite picture." I turn to the page where my mother and her best friend are posed in their organdy dresses. "When Boris gets the film from today developed, I'm going to paste Jeanette and me right here next to them, and when I'm older and my daughter has a best friend, I'll paste them next to us."

"That's a nice plan," Mam approves. "It's called continuity—a very big word."

"What does 'snubbing' mean?"

"Making someone feel you don't really care about them."

"The way Boris made us feel?"

Mam says, "I'm sure he didn't mean to."

I drape her long hair over my shoulders and look at myself in the dressing table mirror. "I hope they live for a long time in a place where the management doesn't allow children."

"Well," Mam says, "they will for a while anyway, so there's no need to worry."

"I'm not worried. But if I moved away, who would you play Parcheesi with? And read to? And hug?"

Mam tries, but she can't think of anyone. "You'll just have to stay," she says and squeezes me tight.

We rock awhile longer and talk about our day. "I found eight eggs," I say. "Poor Jeanette only found three."

Mam says, "You and poor Jeanette overlooked one somewhere. The bunny left a dozen."

"How do you know, Mam?" I don't let on that I saw the dye package the bunny threw in the trash. I don't even breathe, or I might miss out on the answer I like best in the world.

"Why wouldn't I know, Liddy? I'm your grandmother."

Six White Horses

In the summer of 1947, Lila Bickell took an interest in a salesman named Terrence V. Dennis.

Her brother Hector said, *"Terrence,* for God's sake!"

Hector was thirty-eight, a teller at the Farmers Union Bank and nice enough looking except for a certain hardness of heart that showed up as a scowl on his nice-looking face.

"If I were named Hector," Lila said, "I wouldn't throw stones."

Lila, at forty, was pretty in a careless sort of way that kept people from noticing how small and fine-boned she was, and how generally appealing. She wore any old thing and when she got up in the morning, if her hair misbehaved, she pulled a tam over it and went off to her job at the Quality Shoe Mart about as content as she would have been otherwise.

Lila and Hector shared a home, a yellow stone cottage that had belonged to their parents until their parents died. Hector grew vegetables in the rambling old garden, and Lila raised flowers she put around in the dark rooms to lighten the furniture.

They each had their chores. Lila cooked and shopped, and Hector did the laundry and cleaned the house. At night they read in two chairs by the fireplace.

They might have gone on that way for a long time except for Terrence, who came one day and knocked on the door when Lila was at home nursing a summer cold.

She thought at first she might ignore the knock. "If I were at work," she told herself, "whoever is there would give up and go away." Then she got out of bed and put on a dilapidated bathrobe and went to see who it was.

Terrence V. Dennis was an honorably discharged veteran selling reconditioned vacuum cleaners. He wasn't as tall as Lila would have liked, and he had a mole on his chin that she intended to suggest he have burned off as soon as they were married.

"Married!" Hector said. "You aren't thinking of that, are you?"

Lila replied, "If Terrence proposes, I'll accept."

That was later, of course, after she found out more about him and kissed him in the grape arbor a number of times.

"A great many men my age have died, Hector." In the war, she meant, but she steered clear of the war because of Hector's embarrassment at not having gone due to a punctured eardrum.

"I think Terrence and I can be happy," she went on. "And that's all anyone wants, isn't it? Just to be happy?"

"I thought we were."

"How can we be, Hector? We aren't fulfilled."

Through the rest of June, Terrence showed up once a week at least to take Lila to the movies. On the Fourth of July he asked her to marry him and after that he came regularly to dinner on Saturday night.

On these occasions he wore a nice jacket of houndstooth tweed and slicked back his hair with some kind of tonic that smelled like chrysanthemums. Hector inhibited him, sitting like a bulldog at the end of the table, but after dessert he usually said something noteworthy.

One evening he said, "Four out of five women open their doors wearing pink kimonos."

Lila said in surprise, "Mine is tan."

"Four out of five," Terrence reminded.

After he was gone Hector said, "Have you thought about eating with him day after day?"

"He'll be easy to cook for," Lila said. "He eats whatever I put on the table." She was doing what she always did, which was to hum something catchy while she put away the leftovers.

"Does he read at all?"

"Of course he reads."

"I'd like to know what."

"Then ask him, why don't you?"

By then, Hector had let up a little about the vacuum cleaner Lila had bought without consulting him.

The first afternoon he took on terribly. "*I* clean the house. Why should you choose the vacuum?"

"As a little surprise." Lila brought him his gardening boots. "Do you know who you remind me of? Silas Marner, when he smashed his waterpot."

"Why didn't you call me? You knew where I was."

"He was about to break down," Lila continued, "and then he found Eppie under the furze bush."

"Under what kind of bush have you hidden my Hoover?"

"This is a good machine, Hector, with quality parts. Terrence sprinkled wet sand on the carpet and it sucked up the whole mess with only one passover."

Lila went on humming and storing what was left from

the Saturday night dinner. Hector swept around the table, particularly around Terrence's chair where crumbs of biscuits were strewn like dandruff.

He called out to the kitchen. "Terrence V. Dennis thinks all he has to do to support a wife is knock on doors."

"Well," Lila called back, "that's how he found one."

She hung up her apron and went upstairs to look over the trousseau she was assembling in their parents' bedroom.

The trousseau consisted so far of one white nightgown with flowing peignoir, two ivory-colored slips, shoes both black and brown, a serviceable coat that wouldn't show spots, and a print blouse with roses on it.

While she was trying the blouse on, Hector appeared with a new pronouncement. "You'll be at the Quality Shoe Mart for the rest of your life."

"I might have been anyway," Lila said. "But if that's the way it works out, I won't mind too much. We aren't planning on babies."

"Babies!" said Hector. "You're too old for that."

"Oh, do you think so?" She slipped on the coat. "Well, anyway, I don't want any. I wouldn't make a good parent and neither would Terrence."

"I can't think of anything Terrence would be good at."

"You aren't fair, Hector. You're rude to him, in fact."

"He asks for rude treatment. He's oily, Lila."

"Oily? What does that mean?"

"Slick," Hector said. "He can't be trusted."

"How do you know?"

"It sticks out all over him."

Lila folded the nightgown and the peignoir and laid them again with the ivory-colored slips in a drawer smelling of lavender leaves she had picked from the garden. "You'd better get used to him. We may live nearby." She hung up the coat. "We could live here if you like."

"Here!" said Hector.

"There's plenty of room. He could help with the vegetables."

Lila went off to take her bath. When she came out after awhile wearing her worn-out robe, Hector was downstairs reading in their father's chair.

Lila hunted up the book she was halfway through and sat down across from him in their mother's chair.

"I think you hold it against Terrence that he grew up in a carnival."

Hector breathed through pinched nostrils. One of their rules was that neither of them talked while the other was reading. "I thought it was a circus."

"Oh, maybe it was." Lila leaned forward to do a little housekeeping on one of the ferns banking the fireplace.

"No," she reconsidered, "I think it was a carnival. I remember being surprised that a carnival had a band."

"What does a band have to do with it?"

"Terrence's father directed it."

"Terrence's father sold tickets. You told me that your-self."

Lila explained patiently. "He sold tickets first, while the crowd was coming in. Then he put on his uniform and directed the band." Lila moved around in the chair until her spare frame fit it. "It was interesting really. They played from a collapsible platform set up in the midway to keep things lively. When a crowd feels lively, they spend more money."

Hector said sullenly, "What did Terrence do while the band was playing?"

Lila shrugged. "Lessons, I guess. What other children do." She nibbled her lip. "His mother was the circus seam-stress."

"Which was it, for God's sake? A circus or a carnival?"

"There's not much difference, is there? Except for the animals. And the trapeze artists. Terrence sang now and then. Have I told you that?"

"No," Hector said, as if more on the subject was too much to bear.

"One of his songs we used to sing ourselves. You remem-ber it, don't you? It went like this." Lila looked toward the rug where Terrence had thrown out the wet sand. " 'She'll be coming a-round the moun-tain when she comes—' " She labored with the melody like a train having trouble going up and down hills. " 'She'll be dri-ving six white hor-ses when she comes—' "

She went through all the verses, the one about killing the red rooster and all the rest, and then she was quiet.

Hector revived slowly. "Terrence sang that? To a crowd who paid money to get on a Ferris wheel?"

Lila shifted her glance to Niagara Falls, confined in a black frame since 1920. "He did very well, I think, standing up singing in front of people who were eating and talking and not paying attention."

She looked again at Hector. "What do you think of when you hear those words?"

"I don't think of anything. They bore me senseless."

"I think of us when we were children. We never had celebrations."

"We were too poor for celebrations," Hector replied. "The whole world was poor."

"The woman in the song wasn't. Or if she was, it didn't matter." Lila's gaze glazed over with dreamy absorption. "She was just jouncing along in that empty wagon, rushing into town, rushing toward excitement."

Hector scowled. "What empty wagon?"

"The one the horses are pulling. Can't you hear it rattling?" She looked brightly at Hector slumped in his chair.

"Everything to fill it is waiting ahead. Like in marriage," she said.

He burst out suddenly, "I hate this damned business with Terrence V. Dennis!"

"Yes. Why is that?" She peered at him closely. "Is it because I'm your sister and you feel you ought to protect me? Or because when I'm married you'll be discommoded?"

She blew out her breath in a despairing little puff. "It's both, I suspect—though I've never been sure just how much you care for me."

"What do you mean by that?" Hector asked tensely.

"Oh, it's not your fault. No one in this house was ever demonstrative."

She flung out something else as carelessly as a dropped handkerchief. "Our parents never kissed. Have you thought about that?"

Hector got to his feet. "I'm going to bed."

"Oh, do sit down. You ought not to run off when we're finally getting to something."

"Getting to what?"

"To sex," Lila said. "That's why I'm marrying, you know. To experience sex." She watched him sink down again. "Well, haven't *you* ever wanted to?"

"This is not a topic I care to discuss."

Lila said peevishly, "You didn't shy away from it when

you showed me those horses—the ones across the creek that we watched through the fence."

"That was thirty years ago!" Hector said in astonishment.

"I know when it was. I remember everything about it—and it's not a happy prospect, realizing I could go to the grave knowing only about horses."

Hector closed his eyes. "Do I owe all this to a summer cold?"

"Terrence would have come along anyway," Lila said. "He was just slow turning up because of the war." She saw Hector flinch and went on more strongly. "That's something else, Hector. We've tiptoed too long around the war."

"For pity's sake, Lila!"

"You were classified 4-F for a legitimate reason. You aren't a coward who has to slink around ashamed for the rest of your life."

"This is worse than the Johnstown Flood!"

"You're making it worse," Lila told him crossly. "But why not, I suppose? Look how we've lived—like two dill pickles shut up in a jar."

Lila brooded with her chin in her hand. "If it hadn't been for Terrence prying the lid off, we might have had a blow-up instead of this civilized conversation."

"Our *life* is civilized because we don't have conversations."

"We're opening locked closets, Hector." Lila gazed dispiritedly at the pale line of his lips. "The trouble is, most of them are empty."

"You can't possibly judge the extent of my experience!"

"When would you have managed any?" Lila asked. "In all your life you've spent three nights away from this house. Two for your tonsils and that one other time when you camped on the river and the bears chased you home."

"It was coyotes, dammit!" Hector leaped from his chair. "You think you know so much. You don't even know that a man and a woman don't necessarily require darkness."

Lila sighed. "If you know it, I know it. We've read the same books."

The following Saturday while Lila was stuffing cabbage for Terrence's dinner, Hector went out in the back garden and ripped up a pear tree. He left a hole the size of an icebox where the roots had been, and green ruined fruit all over the lawn.

"Our tree!" cried Lila when she stepped out at five to pick mint for the tea. "What's the matter with you, Hector? Are you having a breakdown?"

Hector lay on his back, panting like a lizard. "Can't a man hate pears?"

"You never hated them before. What about in pear marmalade?"

"The worst thing in the world is pear marmalade."

The week after that, he took to wearing red socks and calling up girls.

On Saturday evening he sailed through the kitchen at five minutes to five. "Tell Terrence I'm bowling," he said to Lila.

"I will," said Lila, watching him go. "If he happens to ask, that's just what I'll say."

Hector continued his Saturday night absences. Summer wore down and fall came on before he perceived that the situation with Terrence had altered somehow.

The first thing he noticed was Lila going to work in her serviceable coat. Next he was dripped on by an ivory-colored slip drying in the bathroom. Then he spotted the print blouse with the roses on it laid out for pressing.

He said to Lila, "What's happened to Terrence?"

"Nothing that I know of." Lila hummed. She was putting away meat loaf and *au gratin* potatoes with nice little beans out of Hector's garden.

"You're wearing your trousseau."

"Yes," she said. She didn't explain. She went off upstairs and ran enough water to drown a crocodile. When she came down again, she had on her lace nightgown and matching peignoir.

She smiled at Hector, owlish by the fire, and then at the pear logs, smoking and popping. "Have you seen my book?"

"Your book!" said Hector. "I want to hear about Terrence."

"Oh," said Lila. She took her time sitting down in her mother's chair. "He's off in Oklahoma selling Watkins vanilla."

"Since when?" Hector asked.

"Since the last week in August."

"Well, you might have mentioned it!" Hector recalled wrenchingly the Saturday nights wasted eating restaurant stew and hanging around pool halls until the coast was clear. "Is he gone for good?"

"Yes," said Lila.

He could scarcely believe it. Terrence was gone! In deference to Lila in her celebration raiment with nothing to celebrate, he summoned his scowl. "It's too bad," he said. "The dolt threw you over. But of course he would, anybody fool enough to wear tweed in the summer."

Lila cleared her throat lightly. "He didn't read either— only the funnies."

Hector observed her. She was lovely in white—like a

slice of angel food cake—and not at all dampened by her sad experience.

"What was the *V* for?" he brought out of nowhere.

"Victor," said Lila. She consulted the ceiling. "Or perhaps it was Vincent. Or Vernon or Virgil."

Hector stared at her, pop-eyed. "You never asked?"

"I intended to once. But he wasn't around."

"Well," said Hector. "It was plain from the start he had nothing to offer."

"Plain to you maybe. You have a man's eye for things." A piece of bright hair tumbled over her shoulder. "To me he seemed interesting. He grew up in a circus."

"In a carnival, Lila."

"Whatever it was, he had a very good childhood. He was out in the world, having adventures."

"Now he's selling vanilla. In Oklahoma."

The hall floor creaked. Geese gabbled in the sky.

"I should tell you, Hector." Lila looked toward Niagara in its tame black frame. "Terrence is gone because I asked him to go."

"You ran him off, Lila?" Hector's neck bowed forward. "When you were so bent on marrying him?"

"I was bent on fulfillment."

"It's the same thing, isn't it?"

"It's not the same thing at all."

Hector sat still. Once in a fall on the stairs he was knocked unconscious. The way he felt now, he was just coming to.

"Lila," he said after a suitable pause. "If you've sent Terrence off, you realize, don't you, that you'll have to forget—whatever you hoped for."

"Maybe," said Lila. She twiddled with her hair. "Or maybe I'll find it somewhere else."

The room heaved gently, like the sealed-down crust of a steam-filled pie. "Where?" he said.

"Wherever it is."

She rearranged her white skirts, revealing to Hector's numbed gaze a number of pink toes and pink painted toe-nails.

"Terrence," he said. "Terrence upset things."

"He did," Lila said as softly and smoothly as if she were slipping on slippers at the Quality Shoe Mart. "But he cleared the air too. We can be grateful for that."

Hector shuddered. "Grateful to Terrence." He had breathed ether once. It was nothing to this.

Finally he said, "It's too late, I suppose, to back up and start over."

Lila smiled on him kindly. "It was too late for that when you hacked down the pear tree."

Living

Amos wondered what day, what year the shed fell down. It was true the last time he looked the roof had pitched forward a little, and there might have been a buckling in the west wall, but the framework was definitely standing. Now there was nothing but a pile of kindling topped by a preening mockingbird.

From the porch of the shack his cloudy gaze moved toward the fence and fixed on spindly wands of toad's flax waving in Lura's flower bed. Nasturtiums grew there once, and Dutchman's pipe had twined the pickets. In season, zinnias flamed beside red phlox. Mottled masses of calendulas, sweet peas, pansies, and verbena tossed their scents into the wind.

Lura planted by the moon, and everything grew.

The bin in the kitchen was never empty of potatoes. Spring and fall, dandelion greens simmered in a kettle on the stove beside carrots bursting orange, and cabbage laced with green onion tips and a spoonful of sugar, to be certain —she told him—that afterward they didn't bloat.

Green beans, sauerkraut, beets, and corn gleamed in jars along the storeroom shelves. On the back porch dangled strings of peppers, garlic, and onions drying; and boxes on the floor were liable to hold on any summer day toma- toes, cucumbers, bell peppers, okra, and yellow squash all jumbled together, waiting to get the grit rinsed off.

She was a gardener, that woman. And a fisherman, too.

How long had it been since he'd set his teeth in the flank of a big river catfish? By doggies, hadn't she dragged those bullies up out of that muddy water though? And all before breakfast, too.

Amos had a quick picture of her, coming up through the weeds from the river, the sun behind her, and three or four slick-bellied fish flopping on a stringer, her face red and sweaty, her boots caked with mud. He supposed she was fat by then, but he never thought of her that way.

In his mind she stayed the cow-eyed splinter of a girl her pa said nobody'd ever in his right senses marry. Not unless they were hankering for a whittled-off witch instead of a wife. Goddamn old fool.

Silas Brame—the biggest rogue in Webster County. He'd cut more throats than a meat market butcher. A good number of them at the domino table, a-chewing and a-drinking.

One time he'd took a spell and fallen right out of his chair at Mabel's Beer and Game Palace, smack on the floor, his eyes walled back and tobacco juice spilling over his cheek like worm's blood.

"Heart attack!" somebody hollered, and the ambulance backed up to the door and hauled him off to the hospital.

"Drunk," the doctor said, but they kept him a week anyhow, just for spite.

Old nickel-milker. Wouldn't even give Lura a wedding. Only a dollar bill, all dirty, and a piece of sour advice. *Don't do it*.

She did anyway.

Amos was paying on a flatbed truck he used for hauling wood when the spirit moved him, and they ran off in that. Not very fast. It wouldn't go but thirty. But it got them to the preacher and then the ten miles across the river to the shack by nightfall.

Lura wouldn't put a foot inside until Amos chased out half a dozen alley cats from under the kitchen table. They left behind a rabbit they'd dragged in from the field, and he chucked that out too, right past her nose just as she was coming through the front door in her rose-colored wedding suit.

He'd known in his soul she'd go home then. She ran back out on the porch and threw her head over the railing. But after a time she got all right—maybe she thought of Silas—and came back in, white-faced and furious.

Did she tear into *him*!

Who did he think he was anyway, bringing her to such filth? Animals! In her kitchen! And one of 'em dead!

"Git a mop! Git a broom!"

"It's our wedding night!"

"And you'll spend it in a clean house or yonder in the shed!"

They finished sweeping out somewhere around four in the morning. She even made him light a fire under the washpot in the backyard, and in the moonlight they boiled every piece of cloth in the house, from the sheets to his underbritches, and hung them to dry on low-bending oak limbs.

And still they ended up sleeping in the shed.

There'd been mice in the mattress.

"There's mice a-plenty out here!" he'd yelled because he was fighting mad himself by that time and wondering what in hell he'd got into.

"In a *shed* it's all right!" she screamed back, and they went to sleep in their clothes and didn't wake up till ten in the morning.

Right away she commenced again, sending him around the house with a galvanized pail and newspapers soaked in kerosene to put a sparkle on the windows. After that he had to scrub the wood floor and haul out the mattress and burn it, and then if she didn't make him paint the kitchen shelves with the blue he'd bought for the truck fenders!

About mid-afternoon, they had breakfast in the yard under the chinaberry tree, blooming so purply sweet it sickened him. He'd been ready to faint by then, but she was going strong, poking over the coals left from last night's washing, and frying up bacon and eggs like it was six in the morning. Singing even.

"When we gonna rest?" he said when his watch hand got to five.

At that she stopped, lifted her head from the pot she was scrubbing, and smiled all at once like the sun coming up. "After we bathe."

She took him off by the hand then, down through the burdock and the Queen Anne's lace and the blackberry bushes crowding the river path. There were white butterflies, it seemed now, dancing on the milkweed blooms, and up in the sky maybe a hawk wheeling around like a slow-spinning top.

They swam naked.

There was no mud in the river then, no logjams, and

—further down—no government dam. Just clear, moving water, cold around their shoulders. Afterward, on a bed of sand and wild violet leaves, she gave to him with joyous laughter her cool body and her kisses.

She took a shiftless rascal and made a man of him, Silas Brame told his cronies.

Amos guessed it was true. God knows he didn't have a dime or a white shirt or a pocket handkerchief even, before he met Lura. He'd been living in that cabin so long by himself, eating out of tin cans and laying his ear on the radio at night when he couldn't stand the silence, he'd forgot how it was to have another human being around.

She got on his nerves for awhile. He wanted to get off by himself, and he did, saying he was going to shred weeds or out to chop bull nettle. Anything, so she wouldn't come along.

She sat on the porch and watched him go. He wondered now if she'd cried. If she had, she never showed it. When he came home, supper was ready, or there was bread rising, or she was lying on the bed in her petticoat, smelling like rose water.

After a time he got to liking steady work. Clean sheets, good food. He got to caring if the hinges on the doors squeaked or the window ropes broke. He fixed the sag in the gate and plowed up the garden and learned to scrape his shoes before he came inside.

They had a baby.

The river was so high the bridge was covered. They couldn't get to town. Lura gave birth on the kitchen table, the same one the cats had huddled under when they gnawed the leg off the rabbit.

Tears ran down her face like sweat and soaked into the newspaper under her head. To Amos it seemed she was breathing tears instead of air, but nothing looked the way it was. The walls swayed, and the windows opened their mouths and screamed. The light bulb dangling in the space above their heads stared down like an angry eye, unblinking.

Amos had birthed a calf once. The heifer was blind. She'd fallen in a hole and broken her leg. He couldn't get her out before the calf came, so he stayed and brought the bawling, slimy thing forth into his lap. And now it was his son.

Dead, of course. Amos knew that as soon as he saw the cord circled tight under the child's chin and the little purple face, but he couldn't tell Lura, she was bleeding so.

Finally she knew anyway. There was no crying, and she raised up on her elbow and saw the baby where Amos had wrapped him in a dish towel and laid him on the drainboard.

She was different after that, but Amos didn't notice for a good long time. He looked up one day and saw that she rarely combed her hair anymore or put on a dress.

She slopped about the house in rubber boots and worn-out jeans and most of the time she was dirty.

He hated her then for teaching him to be different from the way he used to be and to care about it. He wished she'd stayed with Silas in his unpainted house and left him to himself.

They screamed at each other, and he cursed her, but he never hit her. A lot of men would have, he told her, but she only looked at him with those big, wide cow eyes, and he kept remembering the river bank with green violet leaves under her shoulders, and he wanted to cry.

She got better.

When spring came around again he came home one afternoon, and she was down on her knees planting flower seeds. She'd walked out to the road and hitched a ride into town with a neighbor to buy them. Sweet William, they were. Little seeds, like pepper.

He'd gone into the house with a sigh, thinking nothing would come of that except another disappointment, but he was wrong. The plants sprang up thick as winter grass and bloomed and bloomed. Pink. Red, so deep it was black. Rose and white stripes, solid cerise, velvety maroon.

They got dressed up. He put a blossom in his buttonhole, and they went to church where they hadn't been since the baby was buried. Lura got religion that day. After that, they wore ruts in the road running into church every time the bell rang, but he didn't give a damn. She was back to like she was, and life became a sweet melon, full of juice running down his chin.

That June they had the baptizing in the river below the house. Lura went under, and seven more too, one an old lady with whiskers and long white hair that swam along behind her like snake ghosts.

"It ain't never too late!" she told Amos when she raised up out of the water, her dress plastered against her bones and her old woman's breasts showing through like dried apples.

Amos thought it would take a heap more than a promise of heaven to make him crawl out of that river wringing wet with everybody bellowing on the bank, and he went off with his hands in his pockets and had a little whiskey from a cough syrup bottle 'round back of the house.

There was dinner on the ground. Piles of fried chicken, potato salad, cucumbers and onions in vinegar, tapioca pudding colored pink and yellow and Paris green.

Lura went around shining like a candle was lit inside her, and Amos got scared thinking maybe she was changing into something he couldn't ever catch again. As quick as everybody was gone, he snatched her up and packed her into the house, just to make sure.

A long time went by.

They passed through happiness and came blinking out on the other side, contented. Lura spread. Through her hips, in her breasts. Amos grew a little belly that lapped over his belt and got in the way when he tied his shoes.

Lura made him tithe, and he found out what the Bible said was true. The money kept a-coming. Lura laid a wool rug on the living room floor and bought a butane cooking stove. Amos owned a pin-striped suit for both the seasons, and they got a truck that nearly always ran.

Then a bad thing happened.

Silas Brame came to live with them.

The damned old fool was three-quarters blind and meaner than a sack of bobcats. He got the bedroom, and they took the sleeping porch. He got the chair by the radio and the footstool.

He talked all the time, balls of saliva shooting from his mouth like popcorn and lodging in the whisker scraggle on his chin.

Everywhere Amos went in the house, Silas was there first. Or his voice was. The sound reminded Amos of a shovel blade scraping flint rock. Worse was the whisper of his felt slippers following each other through the rooms like two old moles trapped in sunlight.

The best thing, Amos decided, was to keep him drunk.

Except Lura didn't like it. Finally one day Amos took him to the doctor, and when they came back they had a new medicine, clear like drinking water, that Amos said might make her father kind of drowsy and thick-tongued and maybe a little crazy.

Sure enough, it did.

Amos doled it out privately from a bigger bottle in the shed, and after that Silas didn't give a hang about the radio or which chair he sat in or where he fell asleep. He and Amos got cordial and even took to playing dominos with a set Amos hammered full of filed-off tacks so Silas could count the spots with his dry yellow fingertips.

Just when it began to seem the old coot might last forever, like those two-headed pigs pickled in glass jars for carnival sideshows, he died, sitting straight up in his chair in the middle of the Grand Old Opry.

Lura took his going plenty hard. He hadn't confessed his Savior, so there wasn't a hair of hope they'd ever see him again, a hardship Amos raised a glass to, out in the shed, all by himself.

They began stepping out some then. Lura liked county fairs. She won blue ribbons on her pot plants and enjoyed sitting in the shade of the livestock barns with lambs bleating in the background, gossiping with the country ladies.

Sometimes they rode as far as thirty miles to Putney just

to look at the store windows and have a dish of ice cream. One March Saturday Lura bought a straw hat with a veil that came down over her face and made her look like an owl peeping out of a navy blue cage, but Amos didn't tell her so and paid for it with a couple of five dollar bills the same as if he used them all the time for lighting up cigars.

In winter when the work was slow, they sat by the window piecing jigsaw puzzles on a sheet of plywood, or else, in the middle of the day, lay in bed wrapped together in a crazy quilt, kissing like kids.

Sometimes they crawled in the truck and rode slowly along the lanes, staring out at the lonesome houses of the country people, refrigerators on the front porches and swing chains knotted high against the north wind.

Winter grasses of gray, beige, brown, and russet spiked the roadside ditches. Hawks wheeled above; crows perched in skeletons of trees, black against the pearl sky. From time to time Amos pointed out stubbled rice fields frothed with flocks of geese.

Then it was summer. Winter. Summer again. Amos caught hot-weather flu and coughed for a month. Lura buried a fishhook in the palm of her hand, and the doctor had to cut it out.

They raised a flock of chickens that dressed out forty hens. Taxes on the land went up. Lura put a black rinse on her hair. Amos called her a crow, but as soon as the roots grew out gray again, he bought her another bottle of Princess Mary Renewer and set it on the shelf above the bathroom sink.

A man in a white Cadillac offered them two hundred dollars an acre for their land along the river. They laughed. Afterward, they took the path through the Queen Anne's lace and the dewberries and saw that there were violets growing still, a deep sweet green, on the bank above the water.

All of a sudden Lura was sick.

A knot like a hen egg came up in her breast. Under her arm an abscess opened and didn't heal. It gave her a fever. Every day they stood by the window and Lura raised her arm while Amos held a mirror and they looked at it in the sunlight.

"Go to the doctor."

"No."

"Why not?" But he knew. If no one said it wouldn't, there was still a chance it might get well.

They made poultices out of aloe vera leaves, and Lura tied them to her with a worn-out stocking. She lost her appetite and grew thin as a girl.

She died.

At her funeral three women Amos didn't know and a

boy named Lawrence in a black-checked coat sang a song about the sunset. Forget-me-nots were blooming by the baby's headstone, and a redheaded lady in a polka dot dress cried.

For awhile, Amos went on talking to Lura. He set two places at the table and served up her plate. He slept on his side of the bed.

The church people came out. When they saw what he was doing, they made arrangements to get him into the Autumn Leaves Care Center. The government would pay for it, they said.

Amos let them talk because they had bought a silver bowl and put Lura's name on it and set it in the church to hold Sunday flowers, but when they rode up to get him he held tight to the door facing, and they went away without him.

Once he thought he saw a woman down by the river.

"Lura?"

He followed after her, and while she fished, he sat down to wait under a pecan tree. When he woke up it was sundown and ants were crawling over his feet and mosquitos big as horses were biting his chin.

"Goddamn old fool," he said.

He let the cats come back. One at first, then three and

four. They curled up on the windowsills and licked their fur on the kitchen table. Mice got back in the mattress.

In the afternoon he sat in the shadows on the porch and looked over his property. He guessed there wasn't much he hadn't had. A son. But he got over that.

Right after Lura died he worried that maybe they'd missed a lot, but when he tried to think what, he only saw the two of them laughing in the ice cream parlor in Putney, or he smelled the roses between Lura's breasts or heard the cry of geese.

Still, there was one thing.

If he could have caught ahold of time. If every now and then he could have held it still with his thumb on its throat, just to feel it quiver, to watch that blue-black vein fill up along its temple and see its heart jump scared and foolish beneath skin thin as any tree frog's. There'd be a sweetness in that. One melons couldn't give. And he'd know for once and all just when it was the shed fell down.

Trip in a Summer Dress

Moths are already dying under the street lamps when I board the bus. I have said goodbye to my mother and to Matthew who is crying because he's almost six and knows I won't be back in time for his birthday. I won't be back for the next one either, but who's going to tell him that?

I spread myself out on two seats. I have a brown plastic purse, a tan makeup case, and a paperback book. I could be anybody starting a trip.

The driver is putting the rest of my things in the luggage compartment. His name is E. E. Davis, and the sign at the front of the bus says not to talk to him. He can count on me.

The bus is coughing gray smoke into the loading lanes. I can see my mother and Matthew moving back into the station, out of sight. I fan myself with the paperback and smooth the skirt of my dress. Blue. Cotton. No sleeves.

"It's too late for a summer dress," my mother said while we waited. Before that, she said October is a cold month in Arkansas. She said that Matthew needs vitamins, that the man who sells tickets looks like Uncle Harry. Some things she said twice without even noticing.

We're moving finally.

E. E. Davis is making announcements in a voice like a spoon scraping a cooking pot. *We rest twenty minutes in Huntsville, we stay in our seats while the coach is in motion.* All the time he's talking I'm watching my mother and Matthew on the corner waiting for the light to change. Matthew is sucking two fingers and searching the bus windows for me. I could wave, but I don't.

I'm riding off into the night because two days from now in Eureka Springs, Arkansas, I'm going to be married. Bill Richards is his name. He has brown hair and a gentle touch and a barbershop. He thinks marriages are made in heaven. He thinks Matthew is my mother's son.

She's young enough. She married and had her first child when she was fifteen. So did I, but I wasn't married.

Matthew was born on Uncle Harry's tree farm in East

Texas where I went with my mother after she told all her friends she was pregnant again. She needed fresh air and a brother's sympathy, she said, and me to look after her.

I was skinny and flat-chested and worked after school in the aviary at the zoo mixing up peanut butter and sunflower seeds and feeding fuzzy orphans with an eyedropper. Most nights I studied. What happened was just a mistake I made because I'd never given much thought to that kind of thing and when the time came it caught me without my mind made up one way or the other.

So we went to the tree farm.

Every day while we waited my mother preached me a sermon: you didn't pass around a child like a piece of cake, and you didn't own him like a house or a refrigerator, and you didn't tell him one thing was true one day and something else was true the next. You took a child and set him down in the safest place you could find. Then you taught him the rules and let him grow. One thing for sure: you didn't come along later just when he was thinking he was a rose and tell him he was a violet instead, just because it suited you to.

What you did was you gave him to your mother and father and you called him your brother and that was that.

Except for one thing. They let you name him.

I picked Matthew because of the dream.

All through the night I'd been Moses' sister tending to the reed basket when the queen found him. All night I was Moses' sister running up and down that river bank hollering till my throat about burst. When the pain was over, there he was—with my mother taking care of him just like the Bible story says. Only you can't name a little pink baby Moses because Moses was mostly an old man. So I settled on Matthew.

It made him mine.

There are four people on this bus. There's a black boy in the second seat blowing bubbles with his gum. Across from him are a couple of ladies just out of the beauty parlor with hair too blue, and a child one seat up across from me. A little girl. Scared probably. She's pretty young for traveling in the dark.

I'm not going to look at them anymore. Everything you do in this life gets mixed up with something else, so you better watch out, even just looking at people. Landscapes are safer.

Pine trees, rice fields, oil rigs. I got my fill of them coming back from Uncle Harry's. I didn't look once at Matthew, but I felt him, even when he wasn't crying. He had hold of me way down deep and wouldn't let go for love nor money.

I sat on the back seat. My father drove and my mother

cooed at her brand-new son, the first one in four girls. If she said that one time, she said it a hundred.

Finally *I* said—so loud my father ran off the road, "He's not *your* child! I birthed him. I'm his mother, and I'm going to raise him up to know I am! Now what's the matter with that?"

My mother said, "Count the *I*'s, and you'll know." She didn't even turn around.

I got used to it, the way you do a thorn that won't come out or chronic appendicitis. But it's hard to pretend all the time that something's true when it isn't.

So I didn't.

I talked to Matthew about it. I fed him cereal on the back porch by the banana tree, and I told him just how it was he came about. I took him to the park in his red-striped stroller and showed him pansies and tulips and iris blooming. I told him they were beautiful and that's the way it is with love.

Only I hadn't loved his father, I said, and that's where I was wrong. A person ought never to give his body if his soul can't come along.

I told him I'd never leave him because he was me and I was him, and no matter what his mother—who was really his grandmother—said, I had a plan that would save us.

Then he learned to talk, and I had to quit all that.

It's just as well 'cause look at me now. Leaving. Going away from him as hard and fast as ever I can. Me and E. E. Davis burning up the pavement to Huntsville so we can rest twenty minutes and start up again.

Now here's a town.

That little girl across the aisle is rising up and squirming around. Maybe she lives here. Maybe one of those houses going by with lights on and people eating supper inside is hers. But I'm not going to ask. You get a child started talking, you can't stop them sometimes.

Like Matthew.

The day I said yes to Bill Richards I set my plan a-going. I took Matthew to the park like I always had. We sat under a tree where I knew something was likely to happen because lately it always did, and when it started, I said, "Looka there, Matthew. See that redbird feeding her baby?"

"That's not her baby," he said when he finally found the limb. "She's littler than it."

"That's right. The baby's a cowbird, but it *thinks* it's a redbird."

He was real interested. "Does the redbird know it's not her baby?"

"Yes, but she keeps on taking care of it because it hatched in her nest and she loves it."

"How did it get in her nest?"

"Its mama left it there." I was taking it slow by then, being mighty careful. "She gave it to the redbirds, but just for a little while."

Matthew looked at me. "Mamas don't do that."

"Sometimes they do. If they have to."

"Why would they have to?"

"If they can't take care of the babies, it's better that way."

"Why can't they take care of them?"

"Well. For one thing, cowbirds are too lazy to build nests. Or won't. Or can't." I saw right away I'd said it all wrong.

Matthew stuck out his bottom lip. "I don't like cowbirds."

"They aren't really bad birds," I said quick as I could. "They just got started on the wrong foot—*wing*." Nothing went right with that conversation.

"They're ugly too."

"The mama comes back, Matthew. She always comes back. She whistles and the baby hears and they fly away together."

"I wouldn't go. I'd peck her with my nose."

"Let's go look at the swans," I said.

"I'd tell her to go away and never come back."

"Maybe you'd like some popcorn."

"I would be a redbird forever!"

"Or peanuts. How about a nice big bag?"

When we got home he crawled up in my mother's lap and kissed her a million times. He told her cowbirds are awful. He told her he was mighty glad he belonged to her and not to a cowbird. She was mighty glad too, she said.

I told her now was the time to set things straight and she could be a plenty big help if she wanted to.

She told me little pitchers have big ears.

Eureka Springs is about the size of this town we're going through. In Eureka Springs the barbershop of Bill Richards is set on a mountain corner, he says, and the streets drop off like shelves around it. Eureka Springs is a tourist place. Christ stands on a hill there and sees the goings-on. In Eureka Springs, Bill Richards has a house with window boxes in the front and geraniums growing out, just waiting for someone to pick them.

I can see people in these houses in this town hanging up coats and opening doors and kissing each other. Women are washing dishes, and kids are getting lessons.

Next year Matthew is going to school in Houston. My mother will walk with him to the corner where he'll catch the bus. He'll have on short pants and a red shirt because red's his favorite color, and he won't want to let go of her hand. In Eureka Springs it will be too cool for a boy to start school wearing short pants.

In Eureka Springs, a boy won't have to.

I can see I was wrong about that little girl. She's not scared. She's been up and down the aisle twice and pestered E. E. Davis. She's gotten chewing gum from the boy and candy from the ladies. It's my turn now, I guess.

"Hello." I know better, but I can't help it.

She puts a sticky hand on my arm. "How come you're crying?"

"Dirt in my eye."

"From the chemical plant," she says, pretty smarty. "They're p'luters. They make plastic bags and umber-ellas."

I open my purse and take out a Kleenex. "How do you know?"

"I know everything on this road."

"You live on it?"

She throws back her head like a TV star. "Prac'ly. Fridays I go that way." She points toward the back window. "Sundays I come back. My daddy's got week-in custardy."

She hangs on the seat in front of me and breathes through her mouth. She smells like corn chips. "They had a big fight, but Mama won most of me. You got any kids?"

"No—yes."

"Don't you know?" A tooth is missing under those pouty lips.

"I have a boy, a little younger than you." I never said it out loud before to anybody but Matthew, and him when he was a baby.

"Where is he?"

"At home. With his grandmother."

"Whyn't you bring him?"

"I'm going a far piece. He's better off there."

She pops her gum and swings a couple of times on one heel. "You got a boyfriend?"

"Yes." It's out before I can stop it. I ought to bite my tongue off or shake her good. A child with no manners is an abomination before the Lord, my mother says. That's one thing about my mother. She won't let Matthew get away with a thing.

The child turns up her mouth corners, but it's not a smile. "My mama's got one too. Name's Rex. He's got three gold teeth and a Cadillac."

"How far is it to Huntsville?"

"Two more towns and a dance hall."

"You run on. I'm going to take a nap."

She wanders off up the aisle and plops in a seat. In a second her feet are up in it, her skirt sky-high. Somebody ought to care that she does that. Somebody ought to be here to tell her to sit up like a lady. Especially on a bus. All kinds of people ride buses.

I met Bill Richards on a bus. Going to Galveston for Splash Day. He helped us off and carried my tote bag and bought us hot dogs. He bought Matthew a snow cone. He built him a castle. He gave him a shoulder ride right into the waves. A girl married to Bill Richards wouldn't have to do a thing but love him.

A girl married to Bill Richards wouldn't tell him she had a son with no father, my mother said. And she wouldn't tell her son he was her son. Or a redbird either. She would forget it and love her brother.

We're stopping at a filling station sort of place. The blue-haired ladies are tying nets around their heads and stuffing things in paper sacks. They get out and a lot of hot air comes in. The door pops shut and E. E. Davis gives it the gas. "Ten more miles to Huntsville."

"My mama better be there this time!" the child says, loud and quivery. I had it right in the first place, I guess. Her scare is just all slicked over with chewing gum and smart talk. Inside she's powerful shaky.

"Your mama'll be there, don't you worry." Before I can close my mouth she's on me like a plaster cast. I should have been a missionary.

"She's always late. Last time I waited all night. The bus

station man bought me a cheese sandwich and covered me up with his coat."

"Something kept her, I guess."

"Yeah." She slides down in the seat beside me. "Rex."

I don't want to talk to her. I want to think about things. I want to figure out how it's going to be in Eureka Springs with Christ looking right in the kitchen window when I'm kissing Bill Richards, and Him knowing all the time about Moses' sister. I want to think about Matthew growing up and getting married himself and even dying without ever knowing I'm his mother.

Most of all I want to get off this bus and go and get my baby.

"Huntsville!" yells E. E.

"I told you! I told you she wouldn't be here." That child's got a grip on my left hand so tight the blood's quit running. We're standing in the waiting room with lots of faces, but none of them is the right one. It's pitch dark outside and hot as a devil's poker.

"Just sit down," I say. "She'll come."

"I have to go to the bathroom."

"Go ahead. I'll watch for her."

I go in the phone booth. No matter what my mother says, Matthew is a big boy. He can take it. So can Bill Richards. I put two quarters and seven nickels on the shelf by the receiver. I get the dial tone. I spin the numbers out, eleven of them, and drop my money in the slot.

I see the woman coming in out of the dark. She's holding hands with a gold-toothed man and her mouth's all pouty like the child's. My mother's voice shouts hello in my ear.

"Wait," I tell her.

I open the door of the phone booth. "Wait! She's in the restroom. Your child. There, she's coming yonder."

I can see they wish she wasn't. I can see how they hate Sundays.

"Talk if you're going to," my mother says. She only calls long distance when somebody dies.

"Mama, I wanted to tell you—"

"That you wish you had your coat. I knew it! The air's too still and sticky not to be breeding a blizzard."

"It's *hot* here, for goodness sakes!"

"Won't be for long. Thirty by morning the TV says. Twenty where you're going. Look in the makeup case. I stuck in your blue wool sweater."

"Matthew—"

"In bed and finally dropping off. I told him an hour ago, the sooner you shed today, the quicker tomorrow'll come, but he's something else to convince, that boy."

"Comes by it naturally," I say, and plenty loud, but she doesn't hear.

"Have a good trip," she's yelling, "and wrap up warm in the wind."

When I step outside, it's blowing all right, just like she said. Hard from the north and sharp as scissors.

By the time E. E. Davis swings open the door and bellows "All aboard for Eureka Springs," that wind is tossing up newspapers and bus drivers' caps and hems of summer dresses. It's whipping through door cracks and rippling puddles and freezing my arms where the sleeves ought to be.

If I was my mother, I'd get mighty tired of always being right.

Limited Access

Miss Ettie is not a house person. She works in her yard most days until it's dark enough to go to bed and she gets out again as soon as it's daylight. I'm putting on my coffee and I can see her over there creeping out of the back door in her outfit: rubber boots, knit pants tucked in the tops, a long-sleeved shirt, a wool cap pulled down over her ears even if it's summer.

If she stood up straight she would be maybe five feet tall. But she is bent from the waist, like a street going around a corner. Arthritis, she says.

She blacks out sometimes: digging in her flower beds, eating Christmas dinner with me. Once in the drugstore.

Miss Ettie says: It's constipation.

We don't know how old she is. Clara says nearly eighty.

Another niece, Francey, says eighty-three. There is not much communication between the aunt and the nieces.

Miss Ettie says: They don't care about me. They send their children over here with cabbages and figs. I already have cabbages and figs.

Miss Ettie's yard she keeps shipshape. Around the back she has dewberry vines, persimmon and fig trees, tomatoes, her cabbages. Growing along the south side of the house she has roses, cantaloupe vines that grew from seeds she threw out the kitchen window, portulaca in all colors, and periwinkles. In the front yard purple and white iris grow, and pink verbenas. In April the place looks like an Easter basket.

Under a tree she has potted ferns on a staircase arrangement of boards stacked on lard cans. No grass. If any comes up, she chops it out with a hoe. How does she tend to it all? She crawls around on her knees.

The house on the inside is a different story.

When I go for a visit she lets me in at the back onto a cement porch where the washing machine leaks and she's hung a clothesline the right height to choke you.

Back off in her bedroom the windows are still boarded up from the last threat of hurricane. A cave is what it is, like a shah's boudoir with pillows piled everywhere and bedspreads draping the furniture and a lot of blankets bunched around on a lumpy bed.

The living room she uses mainly to wait for the mail in. The kitchen is a battleground. Open jars all over. Flour sprinkled around. Miss Ettie's radio broadcasts from the drainboard. It picks up two stations: one plays polkas all day, one gives the news, first in English, then in Czech.

Clara and Francey want to give her a TV.

Miss Ettie says: I've got my radio. What do I need a TV for?

Clara and Francey have talked to the welfare woman. They want her in a home. They want her well taken care of. They would see to it themselves, but she doesn't allow them to set foot on her place.

The reason is because forty years ago at the home place in the country Miss Ettie fell out with Clara and Francey's mother, her sister Abigail. The tale has two sides, one common element: Miss Ettie's father's false teeth, kept in the back bedroom after he died.

Abigail off in Hoxley with her husband the barber and her two precious daughters wanted the teeth done away with. Miss Ettie and her mother, in whose house the teeth resided, felt satisfied they were in the right place, on top of the chifforobe where the old man had left them.

Clara says: To spend the night in that room would scare the liver out of you.

Miss Ettie says that Clara is scared of everything and so was her mother.

Whatever the case, the teeth disappeared. Abigail stole them, Miss Ettie says. On a visit one day she slipped them in her purse and dumped them in the frog pond. Miss Ettie's horse drank there and drank up the teeth. They were found clamped to his tonsils when the rendering plant rendered him.

Miss Ettie says: That is the truth.

Clara and Francey say it is nothing of the sort. According to them, the teeth were mislaid during a once-a-year cleanup supervised by Abigail from Hoxley. A big load of rubbish was dumped in the pond. A pig wallowing there hooked the teeth on his snout and wore them back to the house. Abigail, fanning on the porch, spotted the pig and fell off in the fern bed. Miss Ettie's mother rescued the teeth and flung them in a stewpan Clara had set aside for a sixth-grade scrap drive to knock the Japanese kamikazes out of the sky. Clara delivered the stewpan to the scrap heap herself. She heard the rattling inside but paid no attention.

Francey says the whole misunderstanding is pre-nuclear anyway. She and Clara could do a lot for Aunt Ettie if Aunt Ettie would let them.

Miss Ettie says to me: Do what? If I have to see a doctor, *you* can carry me there. Of course I'll pay you, whatever you charge.

She calls me up one day, but not to see the doctor. She

wants to see the government dam built on the outskirts of town. The backed-up water covers the farm where the frog pond was.

We set out late, following the cattle egrets to where they nest in the drowned trees. On the way I ask: How big was the farm?

Miss Ettie says: Too small to make a living. Too big for mules. The land was good for watermelons and peanuts. Her father raised corn and killed himself trying.

Miss Ettie took care of her mother. Without welfare. She sold eggs. She sold cabbages and figs and fat dressed hens. She sold pies and jelly. She ironed and took in sewing. She looked after babies and watched over sick people. She picked cotton. She pieced quilts. She sold off a few acres at a time down to the yard fence. When her mother died, she sold out entirely and bought the house in town.

Nobody helped you? I ask.

I never needed help.

Miss Ettie takes a look at the government dam. She wants to drive right down to the water, but you can't do that.

There's a road, she says. Don't you see it?

I point out a sign. *Limited Access.*

What's that mean?

It means we can't use the road because we're not authorized.

The idea appeals to her. The next morning she tromps

out in her boots and sticks a sign in the verbenas: *Limited Access. That Means YOU*.

Clara and Francey ring up right away. What's the cause of that sign?

The cause is the same reason she won't let the grass grow. One blade makes two and the first thing you know you have to buy a lawn mower.

But I don't tell them that. I say the sign is for dogs.

Clara says: We bought the TV.

Francey says: She'll love it once she gets used to it.

They appoint me to make her see she wants it. I go over after breakfast. She is out in the back forty, picking dewberries in a tin pail.

I say: The girls bought the TV.

Miss Ettie says: You know why, don't you? They've got an old aunt they don't do anything for.

Is there something you'd like done?

Not by them.

I say: What about the TV? Don't you think you might like it?

Miss Ettie says: Could I get the weather on it?

The weather and everything.

I get all that on my radio.

It's no use, I tell the girls. Maybe you can trade the thing in on something you'd like yourselves.

They don't listen. They go over there while she's chopping out clover on the other side of the house and put it in the living room. A man they brought along hooks it up. Miss Ettie is deaf so she doesn't hear the commotion. She doesn't know anything is going on until the antenna shoots up.

Clara hollers, standing close to her car: It's installed, Aunt Ettie. There's nothing you can do about it so you might as well enjoy it.

Francey says: I'll show you how to change channels, Aunt Ettie, if you'll let me in the house.

Miss Ettie says: If it's my TV I don't need you to show me how to work it.

I wait until the smoke clears and then I go over. The radio is blaring. I knock on the back door.

Miss Ettie says: I guess you know they did it anyway.

I say: Let's have a look at it.

She has a doily on top of it and in the middle of the doily is a china dancing doll whose skirt is a pincushion.

Have you turned it on? I say.

Miss Ettie says: I've been busy.

Francey calls up as soon as I get home: I bet she already loves it.

I say: It was really nice, Francey, of you girls to do that.

We want her to enjoy it. She can't read anymore. She

has all that time on her hands. And in the winter when it rains, won't it be a blessing.

I do a few things in the kitchen. Then I eat my supper and go to bed. I wake up about midnight needing something for heartburn. Out of the kitchen window I see Miss Ettie's living room aglow. Fire! I think first. Then I think TV. I don't want to scare her, poking around, but I have to know which it is before I go back to bed. She could be blacked out on the floor. Her hip could be broken.

I knock where I always do and then I go around to the front where the noise is coming from.

She lets me in. She's all tuckered out.

I have company already, she says. She has a gray, fuzzy nightgown on and chartreuse slippers she bought at a garage sale: plastic eyes on the toes and red felt tongues.

She points to the TV screen, jumping with activity.

They're cooking, she says. In the middle of the night.

She switches channels and gets a stock car race. She turns the dial again. A man in a black coat stabs a woman wearing rompers.

If you're okay, I say, I'm going back home.

Miss Ettie says: When do these people sleep?

You can turn it off. I show her how.

They're still there, she says. Back of that window.

No, they're not.

They are. She proves it. She heads off toward the kitchen. I'll take a broom to that thing.

I should explain how it's possible for people to cook in New York and show up a long time later in somebody's living room, but I don't know myself. Anyway, facts don't concern her. She just wants to put a stop to it.

Don't bang it up, I say. We'll unplug it.

I don't want to look at it. I don't want it sitting there.

She'll be up all night, I see, wearing herself out. I go off to the bedroom. Without making a dent in the decor I bring back a Russian shawl, three or four pillows, and a dime store vase with a fake lily in it.

Miss Ettie watches me set things around. Under. On top of.

Hocus pocus, I say.

She looks at her new lounge table beside the Nile River. Okay, she says. You can go home now.

You won't wreck it?

Not before tomorrow, she says. And only the insides. All cleaned out it ought to make a fine coop for a setting hen.

The girls are upset that Aunt Ettie doesn't like the TV.

Francey says: She could at least give it a fair trial.

Clara says: She's a hardheaded old fool. I wash my hands of her.

It's a good sign, I say, that it's still in one piece.

I go over in a day or two, just to make sure. The fake lily and the pillows are right where I left them, but one corner of the Russian shawl is hiked up to clear the screen.

Miss Ettie sees me looking at it. Sparks could fly out, she says. I have to keep a watch in case of fire.

For the next couple of weeks I put up pickles. I get on a bus and go visit my cousin. When I come home again Miss Ettie's yard looks worse than her kitchen. I stand on the curb and I can't hear the radio.

She's died, I think, and rush to the phone.

She's watching TV, Clara says.

Francey says: We really think she is!

I unpack my suitcase and go knock on the back door. Nobody comes, so I go around to the front.

Miss Ettie lets me in. She's wearing her gray nightgown. She's gray all over.

Are you sick? I say.

I'm sick of all the racket that comes out of this box. How long will it be before the bulbs burn out?

I say: What would be the harm in just turning it off?

Miss Ettie says: There's shows every hour. I wasn't raised to be wasteful.

She droops in the mail chair to watch a dogfood commercial.

I sympathize with the fix she's in. There's nothing worse

in the world than a prejudice gone soft. Unless it's a flower
bed chock-full of weeds.

I try to think what to do. Finally I say: It's too bad, Miss
Ettie, about your radio.

What about my radio?

There's all that music and nobody to hear it.

The next morning at six she's out hoeing the verbenas.
The yard is full of polkas and Czech versions of the news.
I go over at ten when she's resting on the steps drinking
cistern water.

Here's some pickles, I tell her.

She squints off toward the firehouse. I put it on low, she
says, and shut the cat in there.

How are your knees? I say.

Stiff, she says. It's a sin how the grass grows.

Twilight

Elsie was dead, and the women didn't come anymore with their wrinkled paper sacks stuffed with piece goods bought on sale and half-used spools of thread and borrowed patterns for her to turn into dresses suitable for Masses and funerals and bridal showers for pregnant girls.

Hardly anyone visited except Katerina Felcher and her brown feist dog.

Hans, seventy-three, puttered in his shop in back of the garage, building birdhouses and Dutch windmills and nailing them to the limbs of the dying hackberry.

The house was a mess, as it always had been, but now it was worse. Junk had piled up so that only trails wound through it. Elsie kept everything. Drawers full of recipes.

Socks with lost mates. She saved scraps of material no bigger than bacon slices. In the dining room alone there were twelve plaster Kewpie dolls with potbellied stomachs, and cracked bowls and birdcages, and dozens of shoeboxes filled with egg carton roses.

"You could throw those away," Katerina suggested. (The poor skinny thing, the poor bag of bones.)

Hans threw away nothing, afraid if he did he might toss out Elsie. She still lingered, he knew, among her possessions. He heard her cough in the twilight, he saw her stretched on the sofa.

"You could throw this away," Katerina said, and pointed with her toe to a cupful of shoelaces.

(Elsie, who sewed for her, had complained, "Even her necklaces don't fit her neck.")

One spring afternoon Hans got in his Plymouth and drove to the cemetery. The stone was in place, and he wanted to see it before he settled the bill.

Riding along, he admired the blue sky, the tender greens of May, the cows and the flowers.

Then he came to his plot. All thoughts of spring flew from his head.

He had ordered a tombstone for two—and the damned thing had his name on it. HANS LOUDENSCHOTT, as big as a boxcar. Elsie's name too. But of course Elsie was dead.

For the first time he knew it.

Elsie was dead.

He stood at the graveside and struggled for breath. Elsie wasn't at home with her socks and her boxes. She was part of this mound with the grass growing out of it. His darling plump wife was as much a bag of bones as Katerina Felcher had ever been!

In a gallop he fled, sinking up to his ankles in gopher holes, plunging toward the car until he clutched the wheel, hardly aware of how he got to the highway.

The Plymouth took him home—to Katerina on the porch, inspecting her dog's ears.

He moaned when he saw her.

Once, years before, Hans went to the pantry with an armload of turnips. Katerina was there, stripped for a fitting. She shrieked when she saw him and jumped behind the sauerkraut, but her skin showed through, and her peach-colored panties. Hans stood where he was and laughed uncontrollably until Elsie rushed in with her mouth full of pins and drove him off with a flyswatter.

Now he was punished.

"Hans!" she hailed him. "Where have you been?"

Sometimes he welcomed her. They shared memories of

Elsie. But Elsie was done for. Finished. *Kaput*. He slumped in the seat. He might die himself from the shock of the business. He had heard of it happening, and with the tombstone to boot—

Katerina came closer and spoke through the window. "What's wrong? Are you sick?"

He smelled the white wine she sipped on the sly. "Am I ever sick?"

"I was only inquiring." Stepping back from the car, she examined a bird's nest. "Aren't you chilly out here?"

He struck off toward the house. Katerina followed, observing the mud that was caked on his shoe heels.

"Hans," she rebuked, "have you been to the cemetery?"

"Dammit, Katerina! Do you have your nose into everything?"

"You could have taken me with you, to say hello to Emil."

"Listen," he said. "Emil is dead."

"I know that, Hans."

"Then how can you talk to him?"

"You talk to Elsie."

"I talk to myself." He slammed the screened door and took a turn through the house, down Kewpie doll lane, through the maze in the living room. All was in place, except Elsie was gone. She would never be seen in her gown on the sofa. Or poking through drawers. Or cooking him noodles.

Hans returned to the door and addressed Katerina. "You'll catch a cold out there. You'd better come in."

She had added more lipstick and puffed on powder. "May Poopsie come too?"

"No, he may not." Hans sank in his chair. "Poopsie has fleas."

Katerina called back, "He has never had fleas."

"What were you picking then? Lilies, I guess."

She bent to her pet. "Pay no attention. I'll be back in a minute."

Hans watched her come in on her rickety legs, in her grainy black stockings. Through her dark wig, patches of scalp showed like bits of a baby.

"You can sit over there," he said.

Katerina sat cautiously in Elsie's chair where the dress-maker's pins working up through the cushion snatched her breath away in the middle of sentences. "Emil loved dogs," she chided Hans.

He sat with his head back, thinking of Elsie.

"Horses, too. But not cats or caged birds." She whistled thinly through a gap in her teeth. "Did you have a nice lunch, Hans?"

"I don't remember."

She gazed at the parcels, the lumpy brown bags, the lace sticking out of a sack from Sears. "When Elsie passed away she was making me a dress. White eyelet with gores. Maybe you've seen it?"

He hadn't, he said. "But I might have seen Elsie a couple of times."

"Poor Hans," she replied and examined her fingernails. "The Widow Meyer," she said, "has a new pair of glasses."

"Spyglasses?" said Hans.

Katerina tittered. "I'm told she makes stews and shares with her neighbor."

"They're full of buffalo meat," Hans answered her glumly.

A cloud passed the window the size of a whale. Katerina jumped up. "I have to go home."

"Sit down," said Hans.

"I can't walk in the rain. I'll ruin my moiré."

"If it rains," he said, "I'll drive you home later."

"Well, maybe in that case." She resumed her seat like a moth settling down. "Shall I make us some tea? Tea is nice in a storm."

Hans gave a great sigh. "I need something stronger."

Katerina said quickly, "Were you thinking of wine?"

"Wine would be fine, except we don't have any."

"Elsie made wine."

"Elsie," he said, as though tolling a bell. "She made strudel and sweet rolls with cinnamon topping."

"And red muscatel. I helped squeeze the juice bags. The wasps bit her, remember?"

Hans blinked and sat up. "There were ten or twelve bottles. What did she do with them?"

"We could try the garage."

"The garage is no good. I know everything in there."

"Under the sink then."

"She kept the rat poison there."

Katerina said nervously, "Well, I know where it once was, but I'm afraid I can't tell you."

He drew down his brow. "What's stopping you? Lock-jaw?"

"It wouldn't be ladylike to reveal the locale."

Hans grinned all at once. "Katerina!" he said. "I've seen your orange underwear."

"*Hans*." She blushed. "It was peach lingerie."

"It was bloomers to me, and I'll never forget it."

"Then you ought to remember where the muscatel is."

Snorting, he said, "If I did, we'd be drinking it, not sitting here gabbing like a couple of fools."

"You could look in the bathroom. Behind the commode."

"In the hot water closet?" He scowled in amazement. "Elsie said that was naptha."

Katerina laughed shrilly. "I was told it blew up."

"It blew me clean off the toilet. Wine!" he exclaimed. "I thought it was blood."

Katerina stood up. "Shall we look at what's left?"

"It might all have exploded."

"Twelve full bottles? You'd be on the moon."

They salvaged four bottles.

"Two for you, two for me," Katerina told him.

"You couldn't drink one."

"I could. I have."

"When was that?" he asked and sat down on the toilet seat.

"When Emil was fired that time at the mill." She perched on the tub rim and swung her ankles. "He went out to the garage and tied a rope to the rafters."

"Do you mean a noose? My God, Katerina!"

"I know. It was awful. I begged him to stop. I said, 'Emil, my dear, what will happen to me? What will happen to Poopsie?'" She put up two fingers. "Two Poopsies before this one."

"What did Emil say?"

"'Hold on to the rope till I loop it up tighter.'"

Hans said in disgust, "That was Emil all right."

"I said, 'Listen, my darling—let's drink a farewell.' But

he wouldn't, you know. He was so bent on hanging. When finally he did, you never saw him so happy."

"He forgot about suicide?"

"Oh, mercy, yes." She rolled back her eyes. "We had a glorious evening. It wasn't sinful either. If you drink for a good cause, there's no sin to it."

Hans studied her eyebrows (painted on). "I had a bad shock today. Is that cause enough?"

The tip of her nose quivered. "What kind of shock?"

"Elsie is dead."

"Elsie. . . . Like Emil."

Hans nodded and sighed. "It was out at the cemetery. All in a flash."

"When it happened to me, I was planting radishes." She got up from the tub rim. "Go sit in your chair, Hans. I'll bring the wine."

She called once from the kitchen where she went to uncork it. "Are you comfortable, Hans? You won't mind a visitor?"

"What kind of visitor? That hound on the porch?"

"The Widow Meyer," she said. "With your car still out front, she'll think you're having a party."

"I'll put the car in the garage and she won't think anything."

"Oh," said Katerina. "What a good idea."

. . .

They drank the wine warm, Hans from a beer mug, Katerina, a tumbler.

Hans sank into gloom and stared at the shadows. Katerina sang, a song about a yellow monkey in a banyan tree. Then "Auld Lang Syne" a couple of times.

"It's raining, Hans."

"It'll stop in a minute."

She wobbled off crookedly to look out a window. "It's dark," she announced.

"It's overcast."

"It's later than eight. It might even be nine. Poopsie," she said. "He hates to be rained on. He's likely to howl if he's left out in it."

Hans tilted his mug. "If he has any sense he's up where it's dry."

"He might howl anyway. Your neighbor would hear him and know I came over and stayed after dark."

"After nine o'clock." Hans rose abruptly and opened the screen. The dog shot past him and ran under the sofa. "Gone," he confirmed. "Got tired of waiting and went on home."

He banged the screen shut and the door behind it and went out to the kitchen to refill their glasses.

When he brought back the wine the dog had crept out

and sat in her lap. Hans shook his head sadly. "I used to see Elsie. Now I see mutts."

"You're exactly like me," Katerina said. "Always looking behind doors, looking for Emil."

"And all the time, the poor man was in heaven."

"Emil?" she said.

"For God's sake, woman, do you think he's in hell?"

Katerina sipped daintily. "Something else could have happened to him."

"Like what?" he demanded.

"Like reincarnation."

Hans sat down.

"The soul," she explained, "assumes a new body." She removed the dog from his horrified stare. "A *human* body. It's heathen to think he'd be anything else."

"It's heathen to think he'd come back at all! Don't you belong to the Altar Society?"

"I was president one year. Flower chairman for two."

"Lucky for you, you kept your mouth shut." Hans laid back his head. "What a damn fool idea."

"It's a comfort to me."

"Katerina, you're thinking if Emil came back, he'd ask you to marry him." Hans pictured it, laughing. "A screaming baby, and you an old lady with your foot in the grave."

"I was thinking," she said, "more about me coming back

than Emil." She held out her tumbler. "Is there any more wine?"

Hans stayed awhile in the kitchen, putting pots out for leaks. When he returned to the living room Katerina was snoring. The light burned down on her synthetic hair.

"Your wine," he said.

She sat up at once. "I wasn't asleep."

"It doesn't matter."

"Have you seen in these boxes?" She had taken two lids off and pulled out a sweater.

"Katerina," said Hans. He sat down beside her. "Do you really believe you might live more than once?"

"Maybe I do." She put out her tongue for two drops of pink that had spilled on her fingers. "I'd like to," she said. "It makes the end less scary."

"Dying?" he asked. "Are you scared of that?"

"Well, of course. Aren't you?"

He took awhile to admit it.

"The nights are the worst," she sympathized. "But with reincarnation you wake up and start over."

He mulled this response. "What's the point if you come back as stupid as you were the first time?"

"Hans," she said gently. "Each time you're wiser. A little

bit wiser." She put out her hand. "Poopsie," she said, "we have to go home."

"It's raining," said Hans. "You'll ruin your moiré."

"Can't you drive us?" she asked.

"I'm seeing fleas on the ceiling."

She studied the rug, green linoleum with roses. "What shall we do, Hans?"

"There's wine left to drink."

She shook her head sorrowfully.

"Once you could have," he said. "And now you can't."

"What should we do?" Katerina repeated.

Hans got to his feet. "We should go to bed."

They lay down quietly, Hans in wool socks, Katerina's sharp bones wrapped in Elsie's comforter. They napped for awhile. Then Hans spoke in her ear.

"Katerina."

"What?"

"May I ask you a question?"

She looked out from the quilt.

"When you bought the tombstone for Emil . . . did you buy a double?"

Miz Purdy and Gene

Miz Purdy was washing. We washed in the yard then. "Gene," she called.

Miz Purdy wore black. Long-sleeved dresses that stopped at her ankles, and flour-sack aprons and black scarves on her head. Miz Purdy herself was the color of curds.

"Morning," I said from the top of the fence. I was eight years old, watching speckled orange butterflies light on the ash, thinking, Poor Miz Purdy, she only has Gene.

Gene was kind and accommodating, Nora said.

"He's not bright," said my father.

My mother, Johanna, thought Gene was sick. "It's TB," she warned when we sat at our table.

Across the wire fence the Purdys ate too. Not where we saw them. We heard their silverware clinking.

"Don't go over there," my mother said frequently.

"Johanna," my father said, "Gene has a deformity."

"He has one shoulder lower, which means TB."

Nora said nothing. She was seeing a man. For the first time ever, as far as we knew.

"*Gene!*" called Miz Purdy. She had her wash in the pot and the fire lit under it. "Come out in the yard. Your mother needs you."

Gene came out with one shoulder lower and his brown pants on and a Sunday School shirt with the collar left open.

He had a head like a pea. That's how I saw it. And brown eyes and thin hair, and one foot he slung out while the other went straight.

"Your mother needs bluing," Miz Purdy told him.

Gene worked at the store. The Red & White on the highway. Sometimes I went there with a list in my hand. *1 small bread, 1 can of tomatoes.* Gene helped me find things.

"Are these the tomatoes?"

"Uh, yup," he said.

Whatever he touched, we washed with soap.

An older son died. He died over there.

"He was shot," said my father, who knew things from town.

Nora said no, Frazier Purdy took poison. She was told that at school. She was my mother's sister, a teacher of algebra who people had faith in. "But why would he kill himself?"

"TB," said Johanna at the same time my father said it. All three of them laughed and then they explained. "He died a long time ago. You were a baby."

"Those things happen," Berniece the cook said while I helped with the dishes. "That Frazier Purdy, he had to go some way."

The bluing announcement upset Gene. He pawed at the ground with one of his shoes. "I'll have to unlock the store and lock it back up. Walk over here. Walk back there."

"I can't wash without bluing."

"Miz Purdy," I said. I was right there above her. "You can have some of ours."

I jumped off the fence and ran to get it. It was none of my business, as my mother said later, but she wasn't there then. She was off pricing rummage for the church circle sale. Before the day got hot, was what she told Nora. Nora was not there either. She was having her nails done to go out with Howard.

Gene was relieved when I brought back the bluing. He went off toward the highway, slinging his foot.

I took a balancing pole (really a stick I found in the washhouse) and walked from the chicken coop back to the ash.

"Look here," said Miz Purdy from down on the ground.

I turned and looked.

"Gene's left his keys! See on the chifforobe? See through the window?"

I fell off the fence.

"Oh, gawd," said Miz Purdy.

I fell in a fig bush where wasps were landing, nosing the figs with their black bullet heads.

"Run!" cried Miz Purdy and threw up her apron.

I broke a few fig limbs and got up on her porch where asparagus fern grew out of a teakettle.

"Are you bit all over?" She came closer to see, showing blotches of talcum powder caked on her bosom.

"I've got a sting on my neck." I still held my stick. Miz Purdy held hers for poking the wash.

"You're bit on the neck? Can you swaller good?"

I showed her I could, but it seemed not to soothe her. "Oh, god-a-mercy. What will your mother say?"

"She isn't at home. Neither is Nora."

"You've skint up your knee. You've tore a *hole* in your

sunsuit." She fanned with her apron. "Is that cook over there?"

"She's at the African Sisterhood. Nobody's there."

Over the fence I could see our house. It looked plainer and smaller, like somebody else's.

"What a day," sighed Miz Purdy. "Well, you'd better come in."

I thought twice about that. If I caught TB I'd have to go to the mountains. But if I had it already, why not go in?

"Lie down over there," Miz Purdy said in the kitchen. "If you was to faint, what would I do with you?"

I was there where they ate. Where their silverware was. It was a big airy room with a cot by the window.

"Does somebody sleep here?"

"Gene," she said. "Gene's nervous, you know."

"Is that what's the matter, why his shoulder is lower?"

"What?" said Miz Purdy.

"Well, it seemed like it was, but I guess it isn't." I sat down at the table. "I think I'll sit here."

Miz Purdy emptied a drawer on top of the drainboard. "When Gene gets the jitters, he quits his bed. He comes out of his room and comes straight in here."

I thought of how hornets do, but it didn't fit Gene. "Maybe he sleepwalks. I have a cousin that sleepwalks."

"It's nothing like that. It's a nervous condition." Miz

Purdy picked through the drawer things: screwdrivers, paraffin, toothpicks, and nails. "Now where is that i-dine?"

"We keep ours in the bathroom." I watched her a minute. "Miz Purdy," I said, "should I run take the keys?"

"The keys, god-a-mercy!" She struck off toward the chifforobe through a hall and a door.

I followed, of course, to look at Gene's room. Sometimes at night I watched him take off his pants there. In the plain light of day there wasn't much to it: a spare boxy place as bare as a dog's plate. Except on the floor was a nose atomizer.

"Does Gene have sinus?"

"A head cold," she said. She let her breath go, like a black bag exploding. "Look at these keys. Just a pair of old rustys that don't open nothing."

"Where did they come from?" We were both disappointed. I had already seen myself opening the store.

"They're Frazier's I reckon. From back yonder when."

"From before Frazier died?" I was filled with excitement.

"When he nightwatched the icehouse. He had all kinds of keys."

"Could I hold them?" I asked.

They came off on my hands, as orange as the butterflies pressed to the ash. "I guess Gene's in the store. I guess he's selling tomatoes."

"More likely eggs." Miz Purdy polished her glasses. "He's partial to eggs. He don't have to weigh 'em."

I stayed for refreshments: dill pickles and cheese, and two kinds of water, some cold and some not. Miz Purdy showed me her house and her wedding certificate and wrapped up my knee in a turpentine poultice.

The first thing Berniece said was "What do I smell?" She came in straight from the Sisterhood, wearing her hat. "You got turkentine on you? Git out in the yard!"

I could see through the fence Miz Purdy still washing so I stood in the dining room and talked through the door.

"I couldn't help it, Berniece. I fell off the fence."

"You could of fell off on our side and saved some commotion." She put her hat in the pantry and brought out the lard. "Got chicken to fry now. Got that Howard man comin'."

"They have oilcloth curtains," I said to impress her.

"Who do?"

"The Purdys."

"We heard about them. What you got on your suit?"

"This? It's a hole."

"That orange," she said. She leaned down to look. "Rust? Is that *rust*?"

"Oh, god-a-mercy."

"Miz Purdy say that?"

"One or two times."

"When you bathe off the rest of you, wash out your mouth."

We had Howard at noon in a seersucker suit. He was shorter than Nora, which seemed like a shame, but she wore her flat shoes so it didn't show much.

"Hello, Molly," he said. I liked him a lot.

"Do you follow the Series?" my father asked.

"He teaches Science," said Nora.

"Oh, science!" Johanna said.

Berniece passed the rolls.

I said, "Where do you live?"

He said, "Down on the highway." He knew Gene from the store. "Gene Purdy?" he said.

"Molly," said Mother.

"Gene has a head cold."

"Law me," said Berniece, going out to the kitchen.

"I thought it was sinus, from the nose atomizer." I said that to Nora. "It's just like yours."

"What?" said Johanna.

"What kind of science?" my father asked.

"They have a cot in the kitchen because Gene gets the jitters."

After dessert, my father and Howard went out on the porch. Nora and Johanna took me to the bathroom.

"Did you eat over there?"

"Or drink?" said Nora.

"Water and cheese and half a dill pickle."

"Oh, Nora."

"Oh, Jo!"

I was quick to assure them. "It isn't TB. It's a nervous condition."

"Better water than milk," Nora said to my mother.

"Anything's dangerous. Just touching a doorknob!"

"I like Howard," I said. It made no impression. "I didn't go because I wanted to. I fell off the fence. I didn't lie on the cot. I sat in a chair. And Miz Purdy took care of me."

"Don't cry," said Johanna. She had me sit in her lap. Nora brought monkey blood and doctored my knee.

"Let's plait your hair."

"Let's get a fresh sunsuit."

Berniece was leaving. We walked out to the street past Miz Purdy's wash all white on the line.

"You sure fixed up dinner," Berniece said to me. "I could of fried two crows and who would of noticed."

"Why can't I go over there?"

" 'Cause Gene has TB."

"He doesn't. He's nervous."

Berniece marched along. "What you want with those Purdys?"

"I want to be friends."

"Be friends through the fence."

"I want to ask them to dinner."

Berniece stopped by a stump that had ants crawling on it. "You want to kill old Gene? He'd slung his foot plum off."

"Miz Purdy would like it."

"Says you," said Berniece. "Do she ever come callin'?"

"She might if we'd welcome her."

"She'd pee in her pants wonderin' what she could talk about."

"Why not diseases?"

Berniece showed her gold tooth. "She be gladder, I tell you, if you leave her alone. She see your mama and auntie do their comin' and goin'. She say, 'Purdy, you lucky, you just got your own business.' "

"Well, I know about Frazier. I know how he died."

"Say you do," said Berniece. "Did Miz Purdy tell you? If Miz Purdy say, it's pneumonia, I guess."

"How did you know!"

Berniece hiked up her hose. "Sons that drinks. They all die of that."

"Was Frazier Purdy a drinker?"
"I seen him tip up a few before he kicked the bucket."
I got close to Berniece. "Do you go in saloons?"
Berniece walked off in her Sisterhood hat.

Signs of Habitation

Mary Ellen came in, untying her scarf, sniffing the air. *Malt-O-Meal*, she thought. *And nearly burnt toast.* She found Steven in the kitchen, eating his breakfast.

"You've fixed it yourself," she half-apologized.

Steven looked at the leaf lodged in her bangs. "You were gone so long I thought you fell in a hole." On a walk once before, a dog had bitten her. He'd had to go to Emergency and bail her out.

"I was looking at a house." She stopped by the table and kissed his bald spot. "A house for Lucy."

Lucy Emerson was eighty, recovering from a stroke, an old cousin of Mary Ellen's stepfather with no relatives left except her sister's grandchildren who lived in distant places and forgot half the time they had an aunt still alive.

"It's that little gray rent house over on Westchester. I didn't go in, but it's perfect for Lucy. Four or five rooms and a heat pump, Steven. I could see it from the street."

Steven poured enough milk to cover his cereal. "I thought somebody lived there."

"An old couple did, but they're gone now it seems. The man used the garage for refinishing furniture, but the door has been down for more than a month."

The shades were down too, Mary Ellen went on. The only signs of habitation were a potted plant on the porch and a welcome mat where a cat liked to sleep.

"A stray most likely." Mary Ellen crunched toast, still in her windbreaker. "The plant isn't worth much. An aspidistra. I wouldn't think twice about leaving it behind. The man probably died," she speculated further. "I imagine his wife went to a nursing home."

"A daughter could have taken her," Steven said. "Or a cousin's daughter."

"Are you saying I should take Lucy?" Mary Ellen laughed. "You'd divorce me in a week if I brought her home."

"No chance she'd come. You can bet on that."

Steven left for his clock shop soon after breakfast. Mary Ellen started her wash and then rang up Lucy at the convalescent center.

"Good morning!" she said, force-feeding cheer to forestall Lucy's grumbles. "How are you today?"

"I want to get out of here."

"You'll be out before long. Have you had your breakfast?"

"At dawn," Lucy said. "Ice-cold eggs. They refrigerate the trays and then haul them down halls from here to China."

Mary Ellen printed CHINA across the phone pad. Poor Lucy Emerson. Eighty years old and loved by no one. "What does the doctor say?"

"He doesn't say anything. He's one of the Willises." Lucy cleared her throat in Mary Ellen's ear. "It's tiresome out here without any company."

When Lucy was at home she turned away company. Mary Ellen dropped by, bearing bowls of egg custard or pots of geraniums that dried up on the windowsills. If Lucy let her in they sat in the kitchen with its stale bread smells and the oilcloth cover stuck to the tabletop for twenty-nine years.

"I'm coming out there today. What time would it suit you?"

"You don't have to come. You have too much to do."

"I have the whole afternoon," Mary Ellen assured her.

"What's wrong with the children? They ought to visit." She meant the nieces and the nephew, all over thirty.

"They have jobs, you know, Lucy. They stay very busy."

"They could spare me a weekend."

"They sent lovely cards," Mary Ellen reminded. "Anne sent a hyacinth. You had an ivy from Eric."

"I know what they're planning. To wait till I die and make one trip of it."

"Oh, Lucy, they aren't." But maybe they were. The last time they were summoned—for Lucy's sister's funeral—they collapsed on the tombstones while Lucy raved on about civilization's bicycle running downhill.

"I have to see to my wash, Lucy. What time do you want me?"

"Not before three. They're irrigating my colon."

At lunch Mary Ellen said to Steven, "What did she mean, irrigating her colon?"

"A big enema maybe." He went on with his pie.

"That sounds so primitive. Like calomel, or bloodletting."

"I bet Lucy ordered it."

"You're tired of her, aren't you?"

"Not especially." He had relatives of his own, one in particular who never called up until Steven got in the shower. "Have you told Lucy yet that you've found her a house?"

"I'm going to tell her today. Do you think I shouldn't?"

"Do what you want, but she's not going to move." Steven pushed back his chair. "She's lived too long in the ancestral palace."

"It was never a palace, Steven."

"It's a palace to Lucy."

"It's a ruin," said Mary Ellen, "and she can't go back there."

They went to the sink with the plates and the glasses. "She can't climb stairs and she can't afford help. She can't bend down to light stoves anymore."

"She won't care about stoves. It's spring, Mary Ellen."

"It's not spring in that house. It's cold the year 'round. It's like a big empty warehouse since she started selling the furniture."

"Is there anything left?"

"A few pitiful pieces. The china's all chipped, the linens are yellow."

"All first-rate once." Steven selected a toothpick and put it to work. "Tell Lucy hello. Tell her I'm coming out soon for a game of checkers."

"Lucy doesn't play checkers."

"She doesn't?" He grinned. "I guess I won't go then."

Mary Ellen timed her arrival for after the juice carts, when the floor was quiet and she could talk to Lucy.

"Why, you're dressed!" she exclaimed as she entered the room.

Lucy normally lay with the sheet to her chin. In the chair where she sat, she looked sallow and shrunken. "I should never wear green." She stuck out black shoes for Mary Ellen to tie. "When you packed my things there was blue in that closet. A brown dress, a rose one."

"But this one looked warmer. Has the doctor finished his irrigation?"

"The doctor," scoffed Lucy. "He made the nurse do it, the poor bungling thing. The pain was excruciating."

"It would be, of course. In that sensitive area." Outside the window, tulips were blooming. "I wish I'd put tulips next to the porch."

"My rectum," said Lucy, "is the size of a child's. An Emerson trait, small bodily orifices." She showed off her mouth and her miniature nostrils. "It had a great deal to do with my never getting married."

"Couldn't something be done about it?" Mary Ellen said, troubled.

"No decent doctor tampers with maidenheads."

Mary Ellen sat down.

"Don't sit down."

"Are we going somewhere?"

"For a ride," Lucy said.

"A ride in the car?" Mary Ellen was thrilled. "Did the doctor okay it? What did he say?"

" 'Get out,' " Lucy quoted.

Mary Ellen laughed. "He has a sense of humor."

"He has the Willis smirk. His grandfather had it and lost his store."

On the walk to the car Lucy hunched in her overcoat and took air through her mouth like a trout out of water.

"Is this a good idea?" Mary Ellen worried.

Lucy sank on the seat and couldn't speak for a minute. "You were always skittish," she managed finally. "Your mother was skittish."

"She wasn't, Lucy." There was jealousy there, an old-time rivalry best forgotten. "Let me strap you in."

"I can do it myself." Lucy brought out her sunshades, black celluloid relics that made holes in her face.

"Where shall we go?" Mary Ellen asked. She thought of the park near the ambulance station. And Westchester later.

"Spin through town, and then take me home."

"Lucy, you're joking. I can't take you home."

"Not to stay," Lucy said. "Turn on the key. Let's get going."

"I cannot take you home."

"I want to look around."

"You're disobeying the doctor."

Lucy's color returned in two orange spots. "I can do as I please. He knew I would anyway."

Mary Ellen could see herself calling the clock shop. "You're being foolish, Lucy."

"I've thought it all out."

"Did you think of the steps? Of how steep they are?"

"We'll go around to the back where the banister is. If I start getting light-headed you can sit me down. It won't be any different from sitting in the car."

"You could harm yourself. Undo your whole convalescence."

"I won't," Lucy said.

"I'll take you next week. The first sunny day."

"It's a sunny day now."

"Another Emerson trait. Bullheadedness, Lucy. If you simply must do this, I'll go check with the nurse."

"The nurse, Mary Ellen, is a sapling girl. She has no idea what I'm capable of."

"I will not be responsible for risking your health."

Lucy opened her purse. "If you're too scared to take me, I'll call a cab."

Lucy Emerson's house overlooked the town. A tall paper sack, about to blow over.

"Go around to the back," Lucy instructed. She got out of the car and clung to the banister. "Frozen," she mourned. "Everything's frozen."

"There's a patch of green here," Mary Ellen said.

"Clover," said Lucy. "Nothing kills clover."

"Are you all right, Lucy?"

"I'll be fine in a minute."

She revived somewhat in her smelly kitchen. "Home," she said, and took off her glasses to look in the cabinets.

"It's too cold in here," Mary Ellen said. "We're going back to the car."

"We're going to the parlor."

Lucy led the way down a murky hall. "The lights are cut off. You can't see the portraits."

Mary Ellen had seen them five hundred times. Ernest Emerson, in all his phases. Until he hanged himself when his cotton mill failed.

"Step carefully, Lucy. There are loose boards here."

"I know this hall. I could walk it blindfolded." She paused at a door. "Here's the soirée room. Before our reverses we entertained here. Upstairs too, where the ballroom is."

"Yes, I remember. Are you getting chilled, Lucy?"

"The floor planks were curved to give us a bounce so we wouldn't crash through when the dancing got lively."

Lucy took the first chair when they got to the parlor.

"Grand Canyon," she panted. It hung on the wall, a depressing depiction, like slabs of red meat in a butcher's display.

"When I'm gone," Lucy said, "I want Eric to have it."

"I'm sure he'll treasure it," Mary Ellen said. "Rest a minute and then we're leaving."

"Anne gets the china. The linens are Rachel's." Lucy pulled in a breath and rattled it out again. "No burglars at least. It's a wonder, you know, with the town full of dopeheads. If they can't find money, they defecate on the draperies."

"You don't have to worry. The police keep an eye on vacant houses."

"That's what they claim, but thieves break in." Lucy groped on a table. "Where are my photos? Are they there on the floor?"

Mary Ellen let light in by raising a shade. "They're strewn all about. What are they doing here?"

"I was going through the box when my spell came on."

"You were here in this room?" Mary Ellen was shocked. When the ambulance wailed, it was straight up noon. Lucy, she'd thought, was taken ill in the kitchen, not off where the phone wasn't, in the wrong end of the house.

"How in the world?" She pictured the hall. "You couldn't have walked."

Lucy said without interest, "I more or less crawled."

"And you managed to dial when you finally got there?"

"*Emerson*, I said, and help came at once."

Mary Ellen sat down on a faded pink chair. "Lucy, how plucky. How brave you are."

"I was taught as a child to keep a cool head. We had a nanny, you know." Her glance roamed the room. "From London, England. And ropes to go down if the building burned."

Mary Ellen shivered. "We'd better go, Lucy."

"We aren't going yet. I want to look at the pictures. If you're cold, Mary Ellen, your blood is too thin."

"It's you I'm concerned for."

"I'm perfectly fine. Ah, here's an old friend." She held out a cowboy. "Rocky Goodnight's brother. Gyp was his name."

"If you catch a cold in this place . . ." Mary Ellen moved nearer. "Is that Emerson Gates? Isn't he handsome!"

Lucy said proudly, "He's holding the light bulb that shone on his birth."

"My goodness, he is. Why did they save it?"

"Why?" Lucy said. "Because his mother had sense enough to know that it mattered."

Mary Ellen searched further among the faces. "Here's somebody lovely." She bent to look closer. The girl was in lace, standing next to a spinet. "What a beautiful smile. Is she one of the Bradley girls, those notable dancers?"

Lucy leaned over. "You fool, that's me."

"Lucy, it isn't! You had black curly hair?"

"I had worlds of black hair. There's a braid in a drawer somewhere around here." Lucy studied her face, the girlish chin, the smooth serene forehead. " 'The Rose of Tralee.' I was given that name by several young men."

"I'm sure they adored you. You were charming, Lucy."

"I was twenty years old. In the garden room. Here, put it away." Lucy drew her coat closer. "It's boarded up now, but you remember it, don't you?"

"I remember canaries." Mary Ellen tried harder. "Large-paned windows. Ginger lilies in pots."

Lucy closed her eyes. "This was a grand place then."

"It's a grand place now. All it needs is a few repairs."

"You're kind, Mary Ellen. You're like your mother."

Flushing, surprised, Mary Ellen stammered, "My mother. Why, Lucy, you never admired her."

"She was married to my cousin for thirty-seven years."

"You were never friends. But I'm touched just the same. I did often wish. I'm sure Mother wished too."

Lucy opened her eyes, bright bits of black against pasty skin. "Mary Ellen," she said, "I'm going to ask you to help me."

Imagine it, Steven! Mary Ellen said later. *Lucy asking* me
—*like the walls tumbling down.*

"What is it, Lucy? What can I do?"

"I've thought of a plan to get the children here."

The crazy old bat, Steven said.

"How can I help?"

Lucy set her small mouth. "Do you promise you'll do it?"

"Let me hear what it is first."

"Call up Eric and tell him I'm dead."

"Now, do you mean?"

"This afternoon."

"Lucy, that's ghoulish, besides being false!"

"They've forced it upon me."

"No. I won't do it. I could never do that."

"You could give it some thought," Lucy urged.

"What would I say when you turned up alive?"

"You won't even be there. You'll greet them in the kitchen and send them in here. When they're all assembled, I'll come out of the dining room."

"You'll give them all heart attacks! I wouldn't be a part of this for a million dollars."

"I wouldn't have asked you if there was anyone else. My sister Cynthia, she'd have done it in a minute."

Mary Ellen recalled Cynthia at their father's funeral, sliding to the ground like a boiled noodle. Lucy, who found him, who cut him down, stood straight as a flagpole and led the prayer.

"It seems to me, Lucy, you've blown up this visit out of all proportion."

"If that's what you think, that's how little you know. I have heirlooms here, priceless things to hand down."

"You have a lawyer for that."

"My bequests have histories," Lucy said. "They require my attention on a personal basis."

"Then I'll call up the children and say you want to see them."

"I'm not going to beg."

"You're letting pride rule your judgment."

"Pride?" Lucy said. "You didn't learn about pride from your mother's example. She trimmed the crusts off the sandwiches she fixed for the ironing woman."

Mary Ellen looked startled. "What if she did? They were never wasted. She used them in puddings."

"She treated the help like guests, and they laughed at her afterward. The more bread the better, that's how servants think."

Mary Ellen stood, trembling. "We'd better go, Lucy. We're about to quarrel."

"I'll tell you something else." Lucy pointed a finger. "I wouldn't give a nickel for a *vat* of bread pudding. Or your egg custards either. I threw them all down the sink."

"You arrogant old snob! You wouldn't know a kindness if it struck you in the face."

Lucy spread her small nostrils. "Are you going to call Eric?"

"Certainly not."

"Then get me out of here. It's cold as kraut."

Steven was snacking in the kitchen when the sapling girl called. He hung up the phone and went back to the bedroom.

"Bad news from the Center."

Mary Ellen stopped reading.

"Lucy's dead."

"Not *our* Lucy."

"She passed away quietly half an hour ago."

"I can't believe it."

"I can't believe she went quietly," Steven said. "I thought there'd be fireworks."

Mary Ellen wept. "I took her back there at five. She was all right then."

He went to the bathroom and returned with water.

"She wasn't really all right," Mary Ellen said. "She was breathing badly."

Steven patted her shoulder. "She always breathed badly. She had too small a nose to get the job done."

"Was it another stroke? What did they say?"

"She made a little sound and that was the end of it. I'm sorry, Mary Ellen, I know you were fond of her."

"She was dying this afternoon and I let her rile me."

"She insulted your mother." He took off his slippers and got into bed. "She was hard on your mother for marrying Clarence."

"I knew she was sick and I got in a quarrel with her. Think of it, Steven. The last thing she asked me, and I wouldn't do it."

"She asked you to lie."

"A lie turned to truth." Mary Ellen got a Kleenex and blew her nose. "Those careless children. She could have died happy if she'd made her bequests. She might have anyway if I'd done what she wanted. If I'd called up Eric and explained to him later."

"You did the best you could."

"I had a chance to help her and I let her provoke me. On the last day of her life I told her what I thought of her."

"You've been telling her for years."

"Steven, I haven't."

"What were you doing when you knitted those bed shoes? When you baked those custards she chunked down the sink?"

"I was doing my duty."

"You were sending Valentines."

Mary Ellen stopped sniffling. "I'll have to think about that."

"Can you think in the dark?" He turned off the lamp. All the clocks in the house began to strike. Eleven times separately in six different rooms.

Mary Ellen listened with her hand on his stomach. "You've got the Waterbury going."

"It's a little bit off. I'll fix it tomorrow."

"Valentines. Really? Do you think she knew? Do you know something, Steven? Lucy was beautiful. I saw a picture today. She was a lovely young woman."

"She was a lovely old woman. Stuck up as hell without ten cents to spit on. What did she say when you mentioned the rent house?"

"We got in that spat. I never did tell her."

"It's just as well. I drove down Westchester after work." Steven paused to yawn. "The garage door was up. The old man was inside, sanding a chair."

Harvest

J ess Earl Mason ran his daddy's black truck head on into an oak tree at seven o'clock on a winter evening but it was nearly eight before the sheriff came up through the dark of the back steps to tell Mayda and Jeeter their son was dead. Their only son, their only child.

Mayda listened blank-faced to the khaki-suited man making his unbelievable announcement. Elder Longness he was called, though his name was Tom. He was the law now, but through the first six grades of the Rhoan's Hollow School where they had gone forty years before, he and Mayda had sat across the aisle from each other. Elder one grade ahead of her, liking her sausage and butter sandwiches better than his own because of the garlic, and trading whenever notes scribbled on tablet paper could persuade her to spare him one.

"How can Jess Earl be dead?" Mayda said. "How can he be dead?"

Before Elder's knock, she and Jeeter had been sitting under the bare bulb that dangled in the center of the kitchen, Jeeter wet-lipped over the fishing equipment in the Sears catalog, and Mayda across the table clipping a recipe for scalloped squash out of the *Farm Journal*.

They sat down again, Mayda like a tire going flat, and Jeeter blubbering, all in a heap.

"He came up from the river around that curve where Joiner's pasture used to be," Longness said. "He slammed into the tree." Mayda heard the grit that had stuck to the soles of Elder's boots grate on the pitted linoleum. "I can promise you, he never felt a thing."

She fixed her look on the third chair standing empty under the light. "Don't tell me he was drunk. He sat right there. We had our supper."

"It was an accident," the sheriff said.

A drip at the sink tapped a pie plate left there to soak. The hackberry rattled its branches at the window.

"Where is he?" Mayda said.

"We took him straight on to the funeral parlor in Gridley." Longness watched her push her chair back. "You can't go there yet, Mayda."

"I'll see if he's dead or if he isn't."

"They won't have him ready till morning."

"Jeeter, get up. We've got to look about our boy."

"Not till morning," Longness said.

Mayda began to cry.

Jeeter slid out of his chair, a frail, pale man in loose-fitting overalls and cream-colored underwear that bagged at the elbows. The glare of the ceiling light beat with a silver sheen on the skin of his head. Longness made a place for him at Mayda's side, but he passed on by and went off into the bedroom. Mayda brought out a handkerchief from somewhere and blew her nose.

"First the dam," she said, "and now this."

Longness, who had skirted Jess Earl's chair and taken Jeeter's, stared down at the catalog. Nothing that counted with Mayda had ever come out of Sears and Roebuck. "It never rains but it pours," he said.

Mayda's gaze probed a pocket of darkness beside the refrigerator. "Him and Jeeter, they were going to have themselves a bait house. You'd heard, I guess. Going to get rich selling minnows and red worms."

Jeeter reappeared in the doorway. "I reckon—" He

looked hard at the table where Elder sat. "I reckon a tire blowed out."

Longness got to his feet. "It could have been the steering rod or 'most anything."

"I can't stand it," Mayda said, "if I have to wonder until I'm dead, too, what happened."

"We'll figure it out." Elder's voice settled like an arm around her shoulders. "There's all kinds of ways once a feller gets to looking."

Mayda pinched onto his sleeve. "He was named after my pa, you know."

"I remember."

"When he was first coming into his teens, Jess Earl looked just like Pa. Like a picture we've still got of him taken down at Flournoy's old studio next to the blacksmith shop when there was that grove of sycamores still standing there."

Jess Randall—Mayda's father—had grown up hard, his land meant more than family to him.

"A man's acreage," he was renowned for saying, "deserves the best. Dress it up like an eighty-dollar mare," he told his sons, "and see how it struts for you."

They didn't hang around to see.

"We aren't farmers," they told Jess.

"To hell with you then," he told them, and Mayda, who

loved the land the same as he did, got the farm. Every-body in Rhoan's Hollow figured she deserved it, putting up with the old man, most especially after her mother died. They looked for Mayda to get from that plot of good, loose bottom loam the two bales an acre Jess was priming it for when he choked to death on a chicken bone, but it never happened. Mostly on account of Jeeter.

Jeeter's folks were fish-camp people. They came out of Louisiana one spring in a broken-down truck and spilled six children out on the river bank. They set up a tent for themselves and a lean-to for their hound dogs. They never paid a nickel in taxes. Pretty soon the young ones were marrying into the county's old families. The one that married the Posthoff girl got himself elected road commis-sioner and built her a nice frame house and kept it painted, too. The oldest girl had a voice like a songbird and went all over the country singing in a traveling choir.

Jeeter mostly watched the river. In a dime store note-book he kept in his overall pocket, he recorded its highs and lows. He knew how many catfish were pulled out of it from Saturday to Saturday and who had hooked them. He knew when the stream changed course the least little bit and where the dangerous sinkholes were.

He was a river man. At twenty-four, Mayda failed to observe that. What she had in mind for herself was a man to farm her land, and children, and two bales to an acre. What she got was Jeeter, and Jess Earl who wasn't quite bright, and more Johnson grass than she ever had cotton bales.

Then one January morning the government men pulled into her lane and named a price for her acreage. Generous, but Mayda turned it down.

"The county doesn't need a dam," she said to whoever would listen. "Nobody wants a lake where cotton was meant to grow.

"You'll see," she told everybody. "The government has bit off way more than it can chew."

For awhile it seemed she might be right. Flags, stuck in the ground by the U.S. Corps of Engineers, fluttered for two years before they fell over.

But the men in business suits came back. The government lawyers met with the town lawyers. Farmers capitulated right and left. Mayda's land was condemned when she wouldn't sign the papers, and the money went into escrow at the First State Bank of Gridley.

All summer and into the fall she rocked on the porch and listened to the saws bringing down the timber that rimmed her fields. Smoke spiraled up from the fires that burned it. Men on bulldozers pushed the loam of her cotton acreage into retaining walls that eventually would hold back the water.

The level of the lake, the newspaper announced, would reach 18.9 feet on Rhoan's Hollow Road. Up to where Mayda's chicken house stood.

Cut off from the river, Jeeter chewed and spat and pored over the newspaper while the water inched up over the bottomland. The Chamber of Commerce forecast five thousand visitors the first summer alone. They were coming with campers and outboard motors, with water skis and a terrible thirst. Jeeter saw where they were headed, and he and Jess Earl got busy hammering and tossing hen boxes out into the dirt and scaring the wits out of the White Leghorns.

"You're turning the chicken coop into a what?" Mayda said.

Jeeter explained.

She saw that he had already set himself up behind a cash register with a cigar in his mouth and a blue and white yachting cap pushed back on his head. Jeeter would catch the minnows. Jess Earl was primed to tend the worms. Their establishment, Jeeter told Mayda, would offer ice-cold beer and souvenir tee shirts and picture postcards of the lake where the land once was.

The sheriff hung around on one foot and the other until Mayda's crying slacked off. Then he said as gently as he could, "I'll take the clothes on into town."

Mayda looked up at him. "One oak left in the whole of Rhoan's Hollow. Left standing by the government so Jess Earl could hit it."

"Jess Earl's church suit," Elder said. "Don't bother with shoes." He said, "In the morning I'll come back for you and Jeeter."

"We can make it our ownselves," Mayda said, and then she remembered they'd lost the truck too.

When Elder was gone, Mayda picked up the recipe for scalloped squash from off the table and folded it until it was no bigger than a square dime.

"I knew there was a day marked down for this, but I never looked to see it. Us still here," she said to Jeeter, "and Jess Earl asleep in the bosom of the Lord."

"He ought never to have got started with that truck."

"You let him."

"You never said not to."

"He thought he could fly in that old black truck." Mayda sat down. "He thought he was riding a big, black bird flapping its wings over the countryside." Her breath hissed through her nose. "Well, I say in the long run he's better off."

"God almighty, Mayda!"

"He never could have looked out for himself, Jeeter."

"He would have caught on to the bait business."

"You think you could have taught him to ring up that machine? When he never learned to write his name so anybody but us could read it?"

"There's a world of folks doing fine that don't pay no mind to books."

"That wasn't all Jess Earl couldn't handle."

"Farming. Say it."

"It's the best living there is."

"Not for me."

"How do you know? You never tried."

"I ain't your pa."

"It was us had the land. We could have made anything out of it, anything we wanted."

"Anything *you* wanted," he said. "What me and Jess Earl wanted, we was fixing to get."

"Money. Money gets used up and then you don't have it."

"Have you got the land?"

Mayda got out of her chair. "We need to be praying for Jess Earl's soul. Get down, Jeeter. Pray."

He stayed where he was. She knelt beside him, her cheek touching the stripes of his overalls.

"Your way," he said. "Always the right way."

She said with her eyes closed, "I'm praying, Jeeter."

She heard him crying, but his voice stayed strong. "You

pride yourself because you always done what they all expected. Your ma, your pa, your Sunday School teacher." He stepped away from her with his hands clenched at his sides. "In my whole life I never pleased nobody with nothing I did."

Mayda got up, pulling the hem of her skirt free from her garter roll. "Are you bragging?"

His face shone wet and spotted. "Me and Jess Earl could have made it in the bait business, but now we ain't going to and that's all there is to that."

A sour-sweet sickness came up in her throat. "You're feeling sorry for yourself."

"I'm feeling sorry for my boy! He finally come up on a chance to prove himself. It took the whole United States government to give it to him, but by golly, he would have showed you—and everybody else in Gridley too. Except for that stinking damn tree."

"I never asked more of Jess Earl than he could do," Mayda said. "He'd have given away your worms by the fistful, don't you know that? And he drank, Jeeter. He would have finished off your iced-down beer all by himself every day of the week."

"He would have owned a business! Folks would have said, 'That's Jess Earl Mason.' "

Jeeter walked off. Mayda heard him in the other room,

and in her mind's eye she saw him narrow-shouldered with his bones poking out of his underwear.

"You think I don't hurt because my son's dead?" she shouted after him.

Jeeter came halfway into the light. "Not a season ever passed that we didn't have a crop."

"A pitiful few straggles is not a crop!" She turned her face to the black windowpanes. "Just one good harvest. I don't see that was asking too much. I don't see that it was wrong to want that little bit out of all God's got."

The people started coming then. Word had got over to Waverly and Mayda's oldest brother came. There was the preacher and four or five ladies, one that had already baked a cake and brought it hot with the icing running off. They kept coming for hours, filling up the kitchen and spilling over through the bedrooms and into the parlor. Mayda remembered that she hadn't put up her sewing and some of the ladies did it for her.

The clock struck one before they took themselves off, trickling out into the yard, pulling the warm kitchen air with them through the wide-open door. When Mayda finally got her nightgown on, Jeeter was asleep, and her side of the bed was cold as any coffin.

She slept too, in a fitful sort of way. Then she woke up.

The coyotes were tuning up in the hollow. She remembered when she was a girl and they did that and then in the morning there would be white chicken feathers like snow all over the ground.

He was wrong, Jeeter. She'd never had her way about anything. She got the land, but what did that come to? She had Jess Earl, and he was flawed.

She dreamed a little dream. She had curls around her face and a long apron on. Under it was a baby, already born, hanging on like a possum.

She woke up with a start, imagining voices scolding her. Plenty of people thought she was stupid, or proud or mean to go on keeping after him, playing like she could see in him his grandfather's chin, thinking clear up to the end that something fine might still spring out of him.

Well, Jess Earl was finished now. He was finished from the day he came into the world, but thank God she hadn't known it. It was good she hadn't known about the dam, too, and about the land going, and good that she'd never wondered until tonight why she hadn't married Elder Longness.

Jeeter made a bubbling sound. She reached out and touched the bony ridge of his hip and felt the warmth rising through the weave of his underwear.

What it all wound down to was the half-acre the house

stood on and the money waiting in the bank. What could she do now but claim it? Or else let the county bury her son. Whatever was left over, Jeeter could have. He could light cigars with it and buy himself a boat and carpet his bait house.

Through the window she saw one star. Venus, was it? It always struck her as funny that stars had names. That spots of light way off in the sky were Mars or Jupiter or Saturn. As if you could buy a ticket and go there. As if, like people, you could come to know them.

She closed her eyes. She was heading off into a long, slack time, she knew. A time full of fits and starts and back-ups and go-nowheres. But later on—

She turned on her side. Later on she might try her hand at red worms.

Standing By

I arrive at the appointed hour, turning off Waterworks Avenue onto Fountain at five minutes to five on an autumn afternoon, a date that has been circled in red ink on my calendar for a month.

On the front porch of the corner house, a white one built in 1921, my mother sits waiting for me, a magazine open in her lap, her attention trained on the spotty traffic. When she picks out my car nosing toward her driveway, she comes down off the porch, hailing me with a wave. But her smile is not the one I am used to. Obviously she is already imagining the feel of her new teeth, practicing the ways she must accommodate herself to the inevitable.

We greet each other with enthusiasm. She is my mother, but she is a favorite friend as well. Her cologne is lemony, her arms are smooth and hairless, always the object of my envy.

"So tomorrow is the big day," I say, giving her a hug.

"D-day." She laughs more shrilly than is her custom. "*D* for dentures."

I am happy to be home. I was born in this house on Fountain Street. Actually, the house faces Waterworks, but since there are two entrances, my mother chose to turn the side door into the front door, enabling her to use Fountain on her stationery. Waterworks, she explained when I was growing up, might have given an unfavorable impression to her friends.

In April of this year my mother turned eighty. I have come home to be with her while she has the last of her teeth pulled. Or drawn, as she says.

"Nothing but snaggles," she has finally confessed, giving in at last to the admonishments of Dr. Fitzpatrick, who has hounded her for years to have them out.

The problem has been that my mother is still beautiful. Her skin and white hair complement each other superbly. Humor brightens her eyes. Her chin is amazingly firm, her expression joyous. Only these last four teeth, disloyal at a time when loyalty means everything, threaten to deny her cherished hope that her looks will last as long as her life.

"Are you worried?" I ask, meaning is she still afraid.

She knows what I mean—and of what. "A little." She smiles wryly. "Who wants to end up like Shirley Temple?"

Shirley Temple the doll. Mine. In the spring when I was home last, we came across Shirley while cleaning out a trunk. Dampness had pocked her plaster complexion. Her hair was a sight. But her pearly celluloid teeth were perfect —indestructibly gruesome in that old child's face.

"You won't look any different from the way you look now," I say staunchly. "Dr. Fitzpatrick will see to that."

We all have our roles in this drama of extraction. I am the Sustainer. Dr. Fitzpatrick is the Executor. Mother is the Courageous Victim. For weeks we have been readying ourselves. On the home front Dr. Fitzpatrick took impressions and issued encouraging bulletins. Mother organized for the siege, and two hundred miles away I trotted from stove to freezer, filling the latter with meals enough to last my husband and two sons a month.

In Mother's kitchen I mix a drink. Mother pours a glass of wine and repeats for me what she told the check-out girl at her supermarket. "You won't be seeing me for a while. Dental work," she said to the girl. I am not told what the girl said to her.

Dr. Fitzpatrick's plan is to pop the dentures into place the moment the snaggles are out—an inhuman procedure, in my view, and one I have argued against from the start.

I make a last pitch. "Wouldn't it be safer to let the gums heal first?"

"Nan." My mother is justifiably annoyed. "It's all arranged."

I realize the question, coming at this time from the lips of the Sustainer, is inappropriate, but I am panicked suddenly. All at once the event is upon us. "On your raw *gums!*" I shudder. "Won't it hurt terribly?"

"Of course it will."

"Then don't allow it! Tell him you want to wait until they heal." I am ashamed to be switching horses in the middle of the stream—at the opposite bank almost—but I blurt out like a child, "You don't have to do everything he says."

"Dr. Fitzpatrick is an excellent dentist. The gums shrink if you wait." Then the clincher. "I won't look like myself."

What can I say to that? We finish our drinks and speak of other things, but into every topic my mother injects an "if" clause. *If* she looks like anything in time for Thanksgiving. *If* it seems worthwhile to buy a new fall dress.

At six we go out for supper, my mother's final public appearance until she adjusts to whatever defacements the new teeth impose. I order a Mexican plate. Wistfully she abstains.

"Onions, Nan," she whispers when the waitress has gone. "I couldn't subject poor Dr. Fitzpatrick to that."

The evening wears on, and she marks off the hours like pencil strokes against a cell wall.

"Tomorrow night I won't feel up to doing this," she says when we go for a walk around the block.

Over a bedtime beer she says solemnly, "None of this tomorrow if I'm drugged."

I sleep fitfully in my old room. My mother is used to living alone and groans aloud with no thought of the alarm she stirs up in my breast. At some awful hour she has a nightmare, but I let her escape by herself from whoever is choking her, fearing that to wake her might be worse.

At six the next morning, four and a half hours before her appointment, I hear her bustling around in the kitchen. When I come out, I find her brisk and cheerful. This is not a day she expects to enjoy, but at least her plans are properly unfolding.

For breakfast she serves bacon and eggs, toast, jelly she has made herself, and orange juice, freshly squeezed.

"Eat up," she advises. "It may be a long morning."

During my wakeful hours I have wondered about the incidence of cardiac arrest in elderly patients. Has Dr. F. checked her clotting time? What if her jawbone shatters?

While I push my eggs around, she ticks off the lunch menu: boiled chicken, string beans, tossed salad with oil-and-vinegar dressing, peach pie.

"If I'm able to take a little nourishment by then," she says, "you can heat me a bowl of potato soup."

She has prepared everything in advance. The dishes wait in the refrigerator under hoods of beaded plastic wrap. There is also baked ham, boiled rhubarb, and a corn casserole. The cupboard is stocked with invalid's fare: oatmeal, crackers and powdered milk to soak them in.

After breakfast Mother goes out in her duster to sweep the pecan borers' droppings off the front porch. She waters her fern and trims the ivy that is looping over the banister into her pot of sansevieria. I tell her I am walking to the store to buy a paper.

"Watch out for fast cars when you cross the highway."

In a few weeks I will be forty-seven years old. Unless before then I am struck down by a fast car.

At nine, when I am reading the paper, Mother comes back out on the porch to stand in front of my chair.

"I hope I don't bleed a lot."

"I'm sure you won't, Mother."

"I bled all afternoon when he yanked out the bottom ones."

She gives me a minute to think about this. "Myrtle Studer fainted when she had hers pulled," she says. "I may faint."

I get up and give her a kiss. "You won't faint." But I wonder what will happen if *I* do.

When she goes back in the house to dress, I move into the living room to wait. Her hair is already arranged. She had it done yesterday at the beauty parlor because that poor man (Dr. F.) will have plenty to do without having to look at a messy head of hair. In deference to Dr. Fitzpatrick's sensitivities, she has also purchased a packet of breath fresheners and polished her brown shoes.

At ten she appears with a leather purse hooked over her arm. She has bathed and smells of powder and her lemony cologne. She is wearing a dress I like, pale green with delicate violet stripes running like ribbon down to the hem, and a silver cutwork pin in the shape of a thistle.

"Lead me to the slaughter," she says.

A block from Dr. Fitzpatrick's office she remembers the breath fresheners on the nightstand in her bedroom.

Dr. Fitzpatrick is in his mid-fifties, tall, stooped, with an endearing air of indecisiveness.

Rubbing his palms together he says, "I've been waiting for this day for fifteen years."

Apparently he has cleared his calendar in celebration. No one else is around. Not even a nurse.

"Alma," he says, "would you like to get in my chair?"

"No," my mother says.

"Come on anyway." He takes her arm. "But leave your purse with your daughter. That's what you brought her along for."

Mother hands over her bag and they vanish through the door at the rear of the room. In a moment Dr. Fitzpatrick is back, fiddling with the thermostat above a jardiniere of ailing philodendron.

"Cool?" he says to me.

"Comfortable," I answer.

He studies the yellow leaves at his feet until a blast from the air vent sends him out of the room again.

I flip through a magazine. From the office there comes a familiar grinding sound. An instrument wheezes. My mother and Dr. Fitzpatrick laugh.

I hear my mother say, "I missed you at church last Sunday."

"I was fishing," Dr. Fitzpatrick says.

Across the street I can see the courthouse square. A broad sidewalk surrounds the old stone building. My friends and I skated there after school. The roar of our steel skate wheels skimming over the concrete must have driven the courthouse clerks crazy.

The grinding noise goes on, mixed with unintelligible murmurs. Staring at the courthouse again, I am reminded that skating was the cause of my broken wrist in the sixth grade. One rainy Saturday afternoon I sailed off the porch on Fountain Street and onto the sidewalk in a one-point landing. My aunt Nora took me to the hospital. Everyone else was off in another town, watching my brothers perform in a marching contest. My mother brought a fishbowl home with her. For a reason I can't recall, we never bought a fish for it.

Fitzpatrick reappears, hands clasped together at the back of his white coat. He rocks on his heels. "Give her a pain pill every four hours. Or use your common sense. Be sure she eats. Orange juice, ice cream. If they don't eat, the blood sugar drops. The pain pills won't work."

"Are you through?" I ask.

"Through? We've barely started."

Another forty-five minutes creeps by. Then suddenly they emerge, Dr. Fitzpatrick with his arm hooked in Mother's. She is jubilant, almost dancing.

"Look!" she cries, baring her new teeth.

"They're already in," I say weakly.

"In—and they fit!"

Dr. F. gives her shoulder a pat. "Don't forget, Alma. They have to come out for ten minutes every two hours. Come back in the morning."

Mother disengages herself and grins into the mirror. "They're beautiful," she croons. "The least little bit crooked, just like my old ones."

"It's the anesthetic," Dr. Fitzpatrick says to me. "Like two martinis. Make her lie down."

At home Mother takes off her brown shoes. She takes off the thistle pin and the dress with the violet stripes and her girdle.

"I wanted to kiss him," she confides. "But I thought he might faint."

"How do you feel?"

"Happy. Very happy. I'd like to sing."

"Go ahead."

"I'd like to sing 'When Jesus Washed My Sins Away.'"

"You'd better lie down."

She sits down on the edge of the bed. "I'm bleeding."

"You're supposed to. You've had your teeth pulled."

"Drawn," she says. "Go in the back bathroom and get that little gray pot from behind the commode. Put some water in it, for when I have to spit."

I do as I am told, wondering where the pot has been all

these years, remembering its icy rim on my bare buttocks when six of us lived in this house with only one bathroom.

I set it down on a newspaper at the side of her bed and lay a towel across her pillow. She stretches out.

"I'm so happy." She sighs.

"Everything turned out fine. I was proud of you."

"I acted like a ninny . . . all my worrying. But how could I know I'd look this presentable?" Beaverlike, she lifts her lip again for me to admire Dr. Fitzpatrick's handiwork. "Thanks for standing by me, Nan."

"My pleasure."

"Pull down the shades," she instructs drowsily. "Go heat up your chicken. At two you can bring me some soup."

I eat the feast she has prepared for me, sitting at the kitchen table, as tired as if I had wrestled in the dentist's chair myself. I look in on Mother. She is sound asleep.

I stand over her for a minute, considering how fragile the illusion of her beauty is. In repose, her eyes sink back into the hollow of their sockets, flesh sags away from her jaws. In the shaded light her skin appears sallow; her lips form a thin line that barely emits a flutter of breath.

While I wait for her to wake up, I walk through the rooms of the house, inspecting their quiet, testing myself against the silence, practicing.

About the Author

Born in Cuero, Texas, Annette Sanford
was a high school English teacher for
twenty-five years before resigning in the
mid-1970s to become a full-time freelance
writer. She has received two Creative
Writing Fellowships from the National
Endowment for the Arts, and her stories
have been anthologized in *New Fiction
from New England*, *Her Work: Stories by
Texas Women*, *Best American Short Stories*
of 1979, *New Stories from the South*, and
*Common Bonds: Stories by and about
Modern Texas Women*. She lives with her
husband in Ganado, Texas.